THE CALIBRATED LIFE

YOUR GUIDE TO REBALANCING THE SCALES OF LIFE AND BUSINESS

EMMA HINE

AND CO.

CONTENTS

DEDICATION

For my hubby, the love of my life, Adrian who taught me that life can be good.

Thank you for always being unapologetically you and showing me that I can too.

For my three amazing daughters, Becky, Charl and Emily, this is for you. If I can do it, you can too!

Live life your way and never ever doubt yourself, you make me so proud, and I hope I can finally make you proud too!

Finally, to my grandchildren, Bobby, Myla and Roman.

Nanny loves you all so much and wants you to continue to shine bright and be the happy, energetic souls you are.

This world is here for our taking, so let's go and get it...together!

Big hugs and lots of love xx

FOREWORD

You know when you meet someone, and you just know that their mission is beyond powerful? When you know that what they're saying needs to be heard loud and clear by so many. Even without being the loudest in the room or fighting to be heard. Well, Emma and this book *The Calibrated Life* is exactly that mission and it's time for more entrepreneurs to rise up and listen to its wise words.

I meet so many business owners daily, it's one of the perks of being over five years into a really successful online business and I am lucky enough to be able to help women uncover how they really need to be seen, totally unapologetically. But as I sit there, flipping through these pages, I can't help but see so many examples of things that not only my clients have done or are doing, but that I've been guilty of doing myself.

It's safe to say when you step into this entrepreneurial space, you often forget that you are still a human being. A human being with needs, with a life to live and with close friends and family around who are all super precious. And let's face it, you probably started on this journey because you craved spending more and more time with them, certainly not less. I know I did. I wanted that freedom. I wanted to treat the people who mattered to me the most. Those precious moments, to me, were and are everything. So, you strive for the next big goal, the next big sum of cash coming in, the next big thing that's going to get you noticed or get you seen as the go-to in your field and you think, *'Okay, this is setting me up on the right path for that life I desire. Maybe if I push a bit harder, dig a bit deeper, spend those extra hours, minutes, moments doing this, surely, eventually it will pay off?'*

Sound familiar?

Don't get me wrong, I think we start out with good intentions of how all this work is going to help us, but somewhere along the way the business takes over and we forget why we really started. As the 9-5 hours creep into the late nights, that little job you're going to do at the weekend as a "one off" and the endless doom scrolling when really you should be enjoying the time with the people in the room at that moment.

It's addictive.

And really, if we are honest, we don't have enough hands to count on the number of times we've had to give ourselves a talking to, in order to not talk shop at any opportunity. But we have to be kind to ourselves here, I think it's totally normal. This job (if we can even call it that) becomes our life. And why wouldn't it? Heck, agencies have multiple staff doing all these jobs we're expected to do as business owners and we have one little old us, especially at the beginning, just grinding away to move one step closer to the success we desire. Our business becomes our baby. And we'd do anything for it. Of course, we would.

But when does that go a step too far? How many times do you question if it's all too hard and maybe just stacking shelves at Tesco would be easier? Yep, we all have those days and it's because really you started this business to fuel the life you want, not take it all away and that's not selfish. It certainly doesn't mean you don't want to make a difference to people's lives. But that really shouldn't be in sacrifice for your happiness and your freedom.

I remember meeting Emma, the author, for the first time, in an interesting zoom conversation that I wasn't sure what way it was going to go. I'd either secured the client by pushing her out of her comfort zone, or she was going to walk away thinking, "cor that was a blunt discovery call". She told me she was the *Happy Business Mentor* and I remember asking her what that meant? She said, "I just want people to be happy in business" and in my normal black and white tone, I started questioning if we could ever be truly happy all the time. I asked her if she was indeed happy all the time and of course she wasn't. How can you be? We can't control what happens on a day-to-day basis. We can't control the things this entrepreneurial world throws at us. Or life for that matter. But she certainly knew how to find that balance, so I got the intention. The desire for happiness that I think we all have. For freedom. And it certainly makes more sense after you've burnt yourself into the ground building up a business that in its own right was and is insanely successful. We crave happiness. We want things to be different. And as we explored what happiness looked like for Emma, we very quickly saw that the thing she really wanted to help clients with was work/life balance. She was fed up with the noise on the internet and everyone looking "busy" and the impression that was being put out there of if you're not busy, you've not made it. I could feel that frustration of wanting people to really reconnect back to why they were doing it and make sure that their businesses were still working for them and not them for grinding for the business at all costs.

She wanted to strip it all back and show people that their business gets to run *their* way in order for them to live their life. Freedom doesn't have to be sacrificed. And she wanted more than anything for people to know that actually, fundamentally, it wasn't that hard to do it, if you are loved, nurtured, and supported to get there and you find your fool proof plan.

I sometimes think we have to remember that we started this business to live the life of our dreams, which doesn't mean we don't have to work to get it, but that's where *The Calibration Coach* comes in, that's where Emma comes in and in turn this amazing book, *The Calibrated Life*.

If we look at the dictionary definition for calibration for a second, it says:

 To make, adjust, or check the setting of the controls with a tool or measuring device"

And I really think that sums up Emma's mission and this book perfectly. It's not about throwing all that hard work away just because it's not providing the life you desire and it's certainly not about carrying on with a lopsided reality of what it really is to be a business owner. It's all about balance. Adjusting those scales to ensure that you are in control of your business and your life. Because it's no good having your scales over-tipped on just business, but at the same time your business isn't going to thrive if you ain't prepared to work at it.

You are in safe hands, because I've witnessed first-hand Emma's strategies and solutions for getting this balance nailed. She has just the most beautiful, easy to understand way of explaining this to people that shows that you can have both. You can have it all. And I guess in a sense that is true happiness. I eat my hat.

We often don't allow ourselves enough time to really think about this process, too busy in the grind, too busy being busy and it so often gets overlooked with the next shiny thing promising you the world. But one thing Emma and I have hugely in common is the desire to help people know they have all they need inside them if they just allow themselves the space to explore it.

In this book, Emma not only explores reconnecting with your purpose, but shifting your mindset to believe it's possible and making the plan to ensure those scales are always calibrated for that equal balance. That doesn't mean they won't tip from time to time, but she's giving you your fool proof plan to ensure you know how to recreate that balance again.

Emma coming into my world as a client was nothing short of eye opening, as she really does get you thinking differently (even after my years of business), about how you really need to remember what matters and why you started. She's inspired me, just by coaching her on her own journey, about how I could live a more calibrated life.

So, stop reading this, and go and dive into the pages of this book. Because we all deserve to live the life we desire, and our businesses are just our vehicle to make it a reality. Sometimes we need that extra little push to remember that we get to be in charge of how our business and life blends seamlessly as one.

Nicki James

CEO and Founder of *I am Nicki James*

INTRODUCTION

You have the exact same problem that I had...you are feeling like your life has no meaning, you feel lost and despite your best efforts you just cannot find your way in life or in business.

The scales are constantly out of balance, and you just cannot for the life of you find the happiness you so desperately long for.

You wake up every day wondering who you are and why your life is not what you want it to be.

You feel like you have no purpose in life, your business is a heavy burden and life is simply boring!

You are constantly wondering where it all went so wrong.

Am I right?

Then first things first well done for picking up this book, well done for acknowledging that something has to change and for taking this all important first step.

You are not alone and what you are feeling right now can be changed, you can change it and I am here to show you how.

When you started your business, I imagine you dreamt of a life that gave you more freedom, both financially and physically, maybe you dreamt of lots of time off to spend with your family or to go on holiday regularly. Maybe you dreamt of buying yourself a wardrobe full of designer shoes or maybe you simply wanted to be able to comfortably pay the bills each month.

Your goal was to have more freedom, you wanted to be able to run your business on your terms, you wanted to be able to spend time with your friends and family whilst your business continued to flourish. You wanted to be so proud of the business, and life, you had built that talking about it made you burst with happiness.

Your business may be financially supporting you right now, but it is not giving you any freedom, you are so tied to it that it feels like a huge burden not something you are proud of. Life has taken a back seat and you feel pretty fed up!

On the outside people see you as a successful business owner and you appear to be doing great but, on the inside, you just do not feel great. It is hard to admit this, it is hard to say I created a business, but I really do not like it.

I get it...I created a 7-figure business and hated it!

But... It's never too late to turn things around, it is never too late to make changes and to create the life you want, I did it and so can you!

You have taken the first steps you have opened this book which means you know that things need to change, you know that you simply cannot carry on the way you are.

That takes guts, so massive congratulations to you!

The reason I decided to write this book was to put it out there that is it okay to say you do not like something you created, it is okay to say you followed a path and did not quite get it right, it is okay to say I deserve more than this.

You see I believe that we ALL deserve to live the life we want to live, we ALL deserve to have the right balance in our lives, and we ALL deserve to be unapologetically who we are.

That includes YOU!

This book will take you through the steps that I went through to turn my business and life around, it will show you how you can live life on your terms and how you can have a business that you love.

I will be taking you through my *5-step Calibration System* that will enable you to find your true purpose in life and more importantly it will show you how to ensure that it remains at the core of your business.

By putting your purpose at the heart of everything you will fall in love with your life and your business, you will wake up excited for the day and you will start to be you again.

Your business will flourish once you are running it your way as will your personal life too, how amazing does that sound?

Hi...I'm The Calibration Coach and I help women in business to rebalance the scales of life and business, to find ultimate freedom and have quantum success on their terms.

After fourteen years in the corporate world, I decided it was time to create my own legacy and I launched my first business, along with my hubby, in 2006. We grew this business to 7-figures, but along the way I lost me, I created a monster and I hated it!

I knew things had to change, I knew I needed to find the right balance between business and life and in 2021 that journey began.

My 7-figure business has been tamed; it no longer drains the life out of me and yes it has meant a decrease in revenue but that was my choice.

I also launched my passion led business as I learnt the hard way that putting profit before purpose is a recipe for disaster, I now use my experience to help other woman in business find their true purpose and to put it right at the core of what they do.

I help women create their own 360-degree legacy and I bloody love it!

Within this book together we will find your true purpose in life and in business, we will dig deep into your mind and pull out all the things that really matter to you. We will throw away those fears and doubts and replace them with kick ass plans that will enable you to maintain the right balance as you move forwards on your journey.

There is no need to pretend life is good anymore as life really can be good and I am going to show you how you get there.

My *5-step Calibration System* that I will take you through works, it is the process I went through to turn my life around and as you will discover throughout this book; I was in a pretty dark place. I wanted to end my life as I was so unhappy yet here I am, just a few years later, writing a book to help you to turn your life around too!

Together we will create your 360-degree legacy, together we will rebalance your life and business and together we will get you the quantum success YOU want on YOUR terms!

I want to make you a promise here but first I need you to promise me something too.

This is only going to work if you let me in, this is only going to work if you are prepared to be honest with yourself and you are prepared to do the work. I cannot offer you a magic solution that just happens so promise me that you will trust the process and do the work, however hard it gets. There will be full on snot bubble, not even the biggest and most absorbent Kleenex will help moments, but you need to run with it. You need to let yourself feel uncomfortable as that is the only way you are going to be truly honest with yourself.

In return I promise that you can realign your life and your business, you can change things and you can find the right balance. The past does not matter, you cannot change that, but you can sure as hell change the future and together, we are going to do just that!

My *5-step Calibration System* will take you through ...

Finding Your Purpose - Finding your true purpose in life and in business, without this you will not know what balanced looks like, you will not know what is missing and why you feel so out of alignment.

Shifting Your Mindset - You need to have the right mindset to move your life and your business forward so we will look at all those limiting beliefs that have been holding you back.

Setting The Roadmap - Knowing what to plan and when is really important, knowing how to build your purpose into these plans is the key difference between balanced and not balanced so this step will show you all of that.

Taking Action - So you know what you need to plan but what do you do with this plan once you have it? This step will take you through all of that, we will look at the things you need to do and explore some of the ways you can do it.

Maintaining the Balance - To keep that 360-degree legacy on track you need to understand what it looks like; you need to constantly review it and you need to recognise when things are not quite on track so you can readjust your scales a little. This step will show you how to do all of this stuff.

So, let's take the first steps together, let's go and turn your dream into reality and remember even when this gets tough, I've got you!

MY STORY

Before we start to deep dive into Step 1, I thought it would be a good idea to share a little bit more of my story with you. I figured that if you are going to truly believe in this process, and truly put your trust in me, it would be a good for you to get to know me and my journey a little bit more, after all it is my life story that has got me to where I am today and had I not experienced the stuff I had I would never have developed my 5-step calibration system nor written this book.

I want to start with a quote. This is something that a teacher said to me when I was about fourteen years old.

 "You will never make something of yourself"

I appreciate I was not the best-behaved student and studying wasn't top of my priorities list, but this is still a pretty cruel thing to say, isn't it?

Whilst finding my purpose this statement just kept on coming to the forefront of my mind and now, I realise that these seven words played a big part in the next thirty(ish) years of my life.

At the time I probably just laughed at the teacher but unbeknown to me this statement had set a thought in my mind that said *whatever the cost I will make something of myself, I will prove him wrong.*

Life continued, I met Adrian (my now hubby) and I became a mum at sixteen. I imagine at this point the teacher was thinking "I told you so" but do you know what I honestly believe that meeting Adrian and becoming a mum at this point was the best thing that could have happened to me. Just to be clear I am not recommending everyone to become a mum at sixteen, it is hard work, but for me it was the stability I needed.

I was eighteen years old when I started my first 'proper' job at one of the UK's largest Building Societies, it was a temporary admin position, and I was super excited on my first day.

The next fourteen years flew by, I worked my way up the career ladder and by the time I left in 2008 I was the Sales and Regulatory Change Manager. (What a title; corporates love a big posh title don't they?)

I was never totally unhappy at Britannia, the people were mostly lovely, and I had gained a whole wealth of business experience, but despite having a lot of control for how my team operated I always felt stifled by the red tape and the office politics. I hated having to ask for a day off and I hated the mundaneness of the same routine day in day out.

Vey cliché but like most people that give up their careers to run their own business I needed more freedom. I wanted freedom to live my life, my way and freedom to do things my way, whenever and wherever I wanted. I am sure you get it as I am sure that these are some of the things you want too!

I still did not feel that I had proved myself to the teacher, I still felt that despite being quite high up the career ladder and earning a decent salary I was still not 'successful' I wanted my own business, I needed some 'things' to show the world (or should I say the teacher) that I had made something of myself.

At this stage the dream was to move to Spain and open a business there, and it **nearly** happened.

In 2006, we (me and my hubby) set up our ecommerce business, we were determined to create a business that gave us the freedom we needed. The first priority was to it to a stage where I could leave my corporate role. I was the main bread winner in the house at the time, so we had to ensure financial stability, but beyond that it was time to create the life of freedom that we both longed for.

After two years it happened, I resigned from my job.

As the years went by, the business grows, we worked a little harder each time to push it to the next milestone and to the next until it finally tipped that 7-figure mark. This should have been a celebration, surely now I had made something of myself; it takes a lot to grow a business from nothing to 7-figures. But to me it was not a celebration, I did not feel happy and proud, I felt exhausted, and I hated my business. I would have swapped my 7-figure business for a much simpler life at the drop of a hat, yet I still kept on pushing and pushing until I reached breaking point.

I started the business for freedom, I wanted a less mundane life, I wanted to live in Spain, and I wanted to be proud of what I had. I wanted a legacy for my children, and I wanted to be able to feel like 'someone'.

Well, none of this happened, all my focus had gone on growing the business, I was working 80-90 hours per week, it felt like the children had to book an appointment to see me, when I went on holiday I took my laptop, I only ever had Christmas Day off and even then, I would check my emails!

The freedom I so desperately longed for could not be further from the reality...I hated my life, and I hated my business.

The really sad part is I hated me too, in my mind I was a bad mum, a bad wife and I was sure as hell a bad businesswoman.

Life could not be further away from the dream.

In December 2010, it was our Christmas peak, we were working crazy long hours and as usual there was no time for anything beyond work. Our youngest daughter, who was eight at the time, ended up in hospital with a broken femur and at the time we did not envisage what was to come, we thought it would be a case of pop her in plaster and we will be home...sadly it was not that simple. They discovered that Emily had a cyst in her bone, and she had to have load of tests, scans, and surgery. It was going to be a long stay in hospital and a long road to recovery for Emily.

Our priority was of course Emily, she was such a brave little girl and there was no way I was leaving her side. But we had invested in a lot of stock that had to be sold and December was our last chance to do this, we had staff and bills that needed to be paid so one way or another we had to find a way to make this happen.

So, we did what we do best, work harder! Adrian was a rock, he was the one in the warehouse from very early in the morning until very late at night, he was the one rushing over to the hospital, in the snow, to spend an hour with us whilst trying to keep on top of everything at work and at home. I was dealing with the admin as best I could from my daughter's bedside, back in 2010 it was hard as the internet was pretty crap back then especially inside a hospital ward. There was no WIFI, so I was trying to connect via a plug-in dongle!

My other two daughters, Becky and Charl were a little older, they were amazing, but it was hard on them too. They were used to us working crazy long hours, especially in December, but this was a whole new level of crazy!

Those few weeks, it reinforced that our business was not giving us any freedom. Never in our lives had we been so tied to something and right there in that moment I could see it. I did not admit it, I did not say it, but I knew it. I knew we had created a monster that I hated.

Life for me was a bit of a downward spiral from there, my time in hospital with Emily had given me chance to subconsciously assess our lives, it had given me the time to reflect on the monster we had grown, and it had given me time to sit back and watch our lives in slow motion. Seeing Adrian working so hard and seeing the children having to fend for themselves was heart-breaking.

But instead of taking action and instead of taking this opportunity to make lifestyle changes we just pushed on... even harder!

The harder we worked, the more money we seemed to have and maybe, just maybe if we kept on pushing it would eventually pay off and we would get the freedom we desired.

By then we had bought a villa in Spain, and we were driving around in some pretty swish cars, we had some amazing holidays (with my laptop of course) and life had become very materialistic. I was trying to convince myself that the next expensive purchase would make it all better... but it never did!

I had found a way to drown out the pain...alcohol and lots of it!

I was a mess...I was unhappy, miserable, obsessed with spending, doing everything I could to avoid people and I was drinking excessively.

Over time it got out of control, I became a horrible person, drunk most of the time and nasty, really nasty. I am not justifying it at all, how I behaved was wrong, but it was all because I was lost, I had no idea who I was or what I wanted but I knew it was not what I had.

I loved my family, I loved them dearly but, in my mind, I had failed them, and they deserved better than me, their lives would be so much better without me in it.

So, I planned my own suicide, I had come up with so many plans and one evening I sat with my wine and my pills, and I was so close. But at that exact moment my hubby walked into the room; it was the early hours of the morning, so I have no idea why he came downstairs, but something made him. Had he not walked in, I would have taken all those pills and I know I would not be here today. My hubby saved my life in that moment, and he did not even realise it.

I made Adrian's life miserable, yet he was always there for me, whatever nastiness I threw at him (and there was a lot) he still wiped my tears and held me tightly; he knew I needed him more than ever even if I didn't know it myself.

I am not sure exactly at what point I started to feel stronger but in 2020, after dealing with the unexpected spike that COVID bought to our ecommerce business I knew something had to change, I knew I had to stop pretending to be okay and I knew that I was now in a much stronger position to tackle it.

So, into 2021 we came armed with a new plan, a plan that was no longer driven by profit but by freedom, a plan that would give us back some time and that would enable us to be free from the ball and chain we had grown.

Within three months the plan had been implemented and my working hours had reduced massively, I was able to take time off and I was able to go away without my laptop, the business was finally tamed.

Now it was the time for me to find me again, it was the time to find out what I wanted to achieve, and to make it happen and in 2021 I launched my passion led business. I had found my purpose in life, and I had found a way to make it part of my life and my business, I had found balance. I had created my *5-step Calibration System* and I wanted to use it to help others do the same.

I do not want anyone to feel the way I did, and I am on a mission to make that happen.

I finally feel like I have made something of my life, but more importantly, I now realise that it is not about proving the teacher or anyone else for that matter wrong, it is about being true to me and it is about living my life on my terms.

My life; My Business: My Choice!

Now I have not told you any of this for sympathy, my story is not dissimilar to many others, but my story is what has made me the person I am today, my story is what has given me the passion to want to help you to change your life and so I wanted you to hear it. I want you to know you are not alone. I want you to see that it is totally possible to turn a shit life into a good one and together we are going to make your life the one you want it to be too!

Whether you are just a little unbalanced or totally out of balance with your life and business, now is the time to take action, now is the time to put you first, now is the time to turn your dream into your reality.

1

FINDING YOUR PURPOSE

If you are new to my world, then my straight taking approach may not be what you expect so I figured it would be worth pre-warning you a little bit about my approach to things before we get stuck in.

I am very to the point, I waffle sometimes, as we all do, but I do not fluff things up. I tell it straight, which is why this book is not as chunky as a lot are, why say it in one hundred words when you can say it in fifty?

Business or life for that matter does not have to be complicated and my approach is very much about keeping it as simple and fun as possible, I will not ask you to do something that does not add any value to anything.

I will totally have your back throughout this entire process so do not mistake my straight-talking approach for not being supportive or caring, I am one of the most supportive and caring women you will ever meet.

My goal in life and in business is to help others, including you, to live a calibrated life hence writing this book so please do stick with it as this stuff really does work!

I promise we will start to do some actual work soon but one last thing I would like to do first is tell you why it is so important to put your purpose at the core of everything including your business strategy.

 She has a 7-figure business she must be happy!"

This is a crazy thing for someone to say but it has been said to me on more than one occasion, people are very assuming that because a business brings in a decent revenue that everything else in life must be perfect.

The reality is this is not true, money, fancy cars and houses do not make you happy, yes, they may make you feel good for a while and give you a great sense of achievement, but they do not give you a true sense of fulfilment.

True fulfilment comes from your purpose, and it is true fulfilment that brings you happiness.

If you live your life and run your business with your purpose at the core you are going to feel different, you are going to have passion and drive which will make your life and your business far more successful.

Your purpose will give you clarity which will enable you to set the right goals and make the right decisions.

With all the right goals in place you are going to have a more fulfilled life, your business will thrive as will your personal life.

Random fact but research shows that people living life by their purpose live longer too!

A purpose driven business is going to bring you far more success and far more joy than one that is purely profit driven.

Remember me telling you how unhappy my 7-figure business made me, well that was purely because I put profit first and I did not give any consideration for my own purpose. I had a growth strategy that worked but it did not work in the way that I wanted it to, it did not work in a way that gave me the freedom I longed for.

When I talk about purpose, I talk about two things

- *Life Purpose*
- *Business Purpose*

Life Purpose – this is all about you, what you want your life to look like, what you want it to give you, it's all the personal stuff, so for me it is things like freedom, family and travel.

Business Purpose – this is what you want your business to give you, who you want to help, the message you want to spread, the legacy you want to leave.

The essential part of making all of this work is balance and this book is going to help you with that.

So now you know how important it is to know your purpose and to live your life with it at the core let's start to dig into step one of my *5-step Calibration System*, finding your purpose.

As we work through this step, I am going to ask you some questions that are going to get you thinking; they are questions that you may not get the answers to instantly but keep digging it will come in time and remember there is no right and wrong answer.

It is all about getting to know yourself, it is going to be emotional as there will be parts of you that you've been hiding from and if you are anything like me, there may well be things you have hidden for years.

Go with it and the most important thing to remember here is that you have to be honest with yourself, I don't want any more of the 'I think that's what people would expect of me' or 'I should do it this way' talk, this is very much about you, it is about your likes and dislikes, it is about finding the real you.

We are all unique and our purposes will all be different, yes there may well be similarities and some crossover but the way you do it could be different to the way I do it even if they are ultimately the same thing. You need to find your way of doing things and the only way you can do that is if you know what floats your boat first.

Grab yourself a pen and paper and let's start digging...

The first one is a biggie; I want you to get to know your life story. There will be parts of your life that have made you who you are today, there will be parts of your life that have shaped your beliefs and often not for the right reasons, remember the teacher who told me I was not going to make anything of myself - I spent thirty years trying to prove him wrong instead of living life on my terms.

I want you to think back to those dreams you had as a child, those passions that you had as a young adult, and I want you to get to know everything about you.

The reason I am asking you to do this is because it will help you to understand who you are and where you have come from. It will help you to remember back to when you felt happiness and when you felt sadness. It will help you to get to know who you are all over again.

Knowing your life story will also help you as we move onto the next steps of my calibration system.

There are lots of other benefits to knowing your life story beyond the context of this book, it will help you with content planning, personal branding and it will help you with PR for example. I love it when you can get lots of value from something and this task really will give you lots of value.

This was probably the hardest part of the process for me but equally I think it was probably the most enlightening too.

Do not be afraid of what you uncover, let the emotions come and remember you need to do this; you need to change your life so keep going and you will get there, I did it so can you!

Here are a few questions to help you but remember these are just guidance to get you started; you may have to go deeper.

- *What was your childhood like?*

- *Did you enjoy school?*
- *What hobbies did you have a child/young adult?*
- *When you left education what were you going to do with your life?*
- *What career path have you followed?*
- *When did you start your own business?*
- *What role has money played in your life?*
- *Do you have hobbies now?*
- *Do you go on holiday?*
- *Who are your family?*
- *Do you have close friends?*
- *Where have your lived?*
- *What does your life look like?*
- *What are your biggest achievements?*

What you are looking to create is a timeline of your life that highlights your key milestones as well as your thoughts and emotions along the way. You need to get to know what you have done, when and why.

As your life story unfolds you should start to see patterns in your life that will help you to find your purpose. You will see triggers that have caused you to react in a certain way, you will see life changing events and you will see moments where you stopped or started doing things.

Remember to look for both the good and the not so good things as both of these have made you who you are today, and both are equally as important and will help you to understand you.

When I did this exercise, I had to keep coming back to it, getting your full story can take some time so you may need to come back to it over and over again over the course of the next few days, weeks or even months but keep going as it will come.

I know you may find this hard, I cried over and over again as I was creating my life story and I will be honest there are still gaps I have chosen not to explore for now. I would not be asking you to do this if I did not believe it was super important. It is worth the effort, as I said right at the beginning you have to do the work, you have to be honest with yourself and that can be pretty god damn scary at times.

Now you have a timeline, you know what you have done with your life so far, I want to start digging into it in much more detail, now we want to get to know the nitty gritty of you. We want to get to know your true purpose and the only way we are going to do that is by digging deep.

Did you uncover any little surprises whilst getting to know your life story, was there something you had forgotten about or something that you had chosen to forget about?

If not then great but before you move on, I would ask you to be 100% positive that you have not missed something out, most of my clients have something, even if is something that is teeny, it is often those teeny things that affect us most. After all, you would wonder how one simple sentence a teacher said to me could have such a bearing on my life? But it did and it was not until I realised it some thirty years later that I could move on from it.

To find your true purpose you have to firstly find you, you have to get to know who you are inside and out and if you are not being totally honest with yourself then you will never quite get there.

By getting to know your own personal life story, you can start to understand you more, you can get to see what you enjoy and what you don't, you can see where your strengths are and where your weaknesses are too.

Your life story will be what has created the person that looks back at you in the mirror every morning, it is your life story that has made you who you are today and now you know yours you can start to shape it for the future, you can tweak it to create a purpose driven life and ultimately you can find your own version of happiness.

Are you ready for a little more digging? Grab that pen and paper again it is time for a few more questions.

When working through these questions think back to those childhood memories, think about the things you used to love doing but have stopped doing. Why did you stop doing them, did you outgrow it or is because other things took over or did you feel they were things you shouldn't be doing anymore?

In my corporate days one of the things, I used to love was delivering workshops. I used to love helping others to learn, I found it enlightening seeing people grow and develop. I loved the interaction with the delegates, and I loved knowing that I had played a part in helping others with their own personal growth. My sense of achievement at the end of each workshop was huge.

But in my ecommerce business this all stopped, there was no demand for workshops, there was no need for group training as everything was done on the job. I spent a lot of my time tied to my desk, so I had minimal interaction with people full stop.

At the time I did not realise how much I missed this inter-action; I did not realise how much I enjoyed being amongst people and how much I loved to help others grow. I never once considered me when I was building my business.

As you know, the rest is history so to speak, the business grew and so did my unhappiness.

It was when I finally started to get to know me again, it was when I started to ask myself these questions and more importantly when I started to be honest with myself that I finally found a way to be happy and to run my business on my terms.

Remember there is no right or wrong answer, you should not be ashamed of anything that YOU want from your life, after all it is YOUR life!

- I want you to think about what you enjoy, I mean every last thing, what lights you up and makes you feel full of life? What gives you so much pleasure you want to do it every day of the week?
- Think about what is really important to you, is it family or travel, is it freedom or love? What are the things that you need in your life?
- Now on the flip side I want you to think about what really pisses you off, what gets you so angry that you could get on your soap box for hours. What makes you want to stay in bed instead of facing the day?
- Think about the things in your life that you hate, the things that you would change at the drop of a hat, what would you give up or change if you could? I don't want you thinking of the reasons you can't change them, just think about what you would change.

By now you should have a lovely list of things about you, you should be starting to get a good picture of the things that you enjoy as well as the things you don't enjoy.

What I also want you to do is look at the list again and make sure you know why you do or do not do the things you have are there; this is for both the fun and the not so fun things.

So, for example if you enjoy going to the pub like me, do you still do it? If not, why not? If you do still go, is it as often as you would like?

I want you to have a really detailed picture of these things as they play a really important part in your purpose so keep digging until you feel you have everything. Do not expect this to all come to you in one go; it will take you some time to get the full picture. I am still coming across things now and it is over twelve months since I started this process but that is okay as it is important that we keep tweaking and changing things as we go.

If you are struggling here is a little tip for you, ask your friends and family. I know that sounds a little bit of a contradiction when I am saying it is all about you but sometimes, we get so lost that we cannot even think about the last time we laughed so hard our sides hurt or we cannot remember the last time we watched something on TV that made us sob for hours, but others will.

Do not push it and do not worry if you feel that you have not got everything as you can (and should) come back to this over and over again.

Right are you ready to move onto the next thing; I did warn you this step takes a lot of digging and can be exhausting but keep with me as it is super important and remember I promised I would help you to realign your life and your business but you had to promise to do the work first...well now is your turn to stick to that promise....it will be worth it!

The next thing I want you to think about is your legacy; what is it that you want to create that you are remembered for?

I know sounds a bit morbid, but it's not.

Our time on earth is limited, we all know that, but that does not mean it has to be limited in the sense that we do not do what we want with it, it does not mean that we cannot create a legacy that makes a difference in some way.

When people talk about legacy, they often talk about the assets they leave behind, the physical things, the hard cash, but I want you to think deeper than that, I want you to think about the feelings and emotions that you want to leave behind, the things that you will be remembered for.

If you could be a fly on the wall in a room full of people who were talking about you what would you want them to be saying?

What impact are you looking to have on people, be them your close friends and family, clients, or total strangers?

Are you looking to change something in the world? Think back to those things that get you so angry you could get on your soap box all day for.

What would you regret if you did not do it? Maybe there is something you already regret that plays on your mind every day?

What would make you feel so much pride if you could achieve it? Even if you could not achieve it the fact that you attempted it would be enough to make you proud?

Remember at this stage we are not looking for solutions, we are not looking for how we are going to do any of this stuff, that all comes later. What we are trying to create here is a full picture of your purpose, your reason for getting out of bed every day and the thing that makes your life so much more fulfilled and aligned.

Before we move onto the next part of my *5-step Calibration System* there is one more thing I need you to do.

We have explored all the things that you want to get out of your life, we know what you enjoy, what you don't enjoy and what legacy you want to leave but we need to make sure that you know all this stuff for your business too.

Now a lot of this stuff will have come up when you were working through all the other questions but there is just a couple of extra business specific things, I need you to ask you yourself, just in case they have been missed

- What is it you want your business to give you?
- What is the reason you started your business?
- What is the message you are trying to share?

This is pretty heavy stuff, isn't it? I do get it, I get that there will be tears, there will be tantrums and there will be full on I cannot do it moments. I suspect you will also think it is a waste of time too, but you can totally do this.

Let me take you away from all these questions for a minute as I want you to come on a little 'imagine this' journey with me. I think it is important to spend some time thinking about your future and I feel now is a good time to do just that.

I want you to close your eyes, I want you to think about your life right now, how do you feel, what can you taste, what can you smell, what noises are surrounding you, what emotions are you feeling.

Then I want you to imagine your dream, think about living the life that you want, imagine having the business that you want, I want you to think about all he emotions and the feelings this is giving you.

Now I want you to be there, be in that dream, stay there for a while. Think about how you feel right now, does it feel good? Can you feel the difference? What can you see, hear and smell, use all your senses? Think about the people that surround you, the legacy you are creating. Let yourself drift off into this new world that you are about to create for yourself.... enjoy it, absorb it!

So come on close your eyes, get lost in your thoughts for a while.

How did that feel? Amazing right?

Now repeat after me:

"That dream is going to be my reality"

Say it again...

"That dream is going to be my reality"

Now every time this process gets hard, every time you think you cannot do it, I want you to repeat this exercise, I want you to imagine how it feels and I want you to remind your-self that YOU CAN DO IT! I did it, you can too.

2

SHIFTING YOUR MINDSET

Well done you for working your way through Step 1; in my opinion that is the hardest step, and you did it!

By now you should know your purpose, you may not have it nailed to perfection, but you should have a pretty good idea who you are and what you want your life and business to look like. You should know what in your life right now is good and what is not so good, and you should know what you want to change.

But before we get stuck into what we do with all this stuff, I want to take you through Step 2 of my calibration system, which is shifting your mindset.

You see your happiness; your success is driven not only by your purpose but by your mindset as well. Even if you know exactly what you want your life to look like, if you are telling yourself, you cannot do it then the chances are you won't.

By changing your mindset, you are going to change your behaviour, you are going to change the way you think and the way you act.

Back in 2021 when I started my own personal discovery journey, I didn't believe that I knew anything that would benefit other people, and even if I did, I didn't believe that anyone would buy from me. I was afraid to be visible. I did not even tell anyone, not even my hubby about the work I was doing as I felt guilty for trying to do something for me. I thought people would laugh at me and think I was just being 'silly'.

I had spent years telling myself that I was a failure and that I was only capable of self-destruction. Remember my story about the teacher telling me I would never make something of myself. Well, that was constantly at the back of my mind, I believed he was right, I would never make someone of myself.

I changed my mindset and my behaviour started to change too, I started to act differently, I started to talk differently, and I found a new self confidence that enabled me to think 'fuck it' I can do whatever I damn well want, and nobody can stop me!

I knew that I could make something of myself.

There is nothing worse than that monkey on your shoulder that keeps telling you that you cannot do something, that you were destined to just plod through life without being the person you deserve to be.

I want to show you how you can stop listening to that monkey and how over time, the more you stop listening, the more he stays away.

We cannot stop these thoughts and beliefs from popping up every now and again, but we can learn how to control them.

So, what is mindset?

> *A set of attitudes or fixed ideas that somebody has and that are often difficult to change"*
>
> — *OXFORD DICTIONARY*

Difficult to change, but not impossible!

Let me tell you why it is difficult to change, it is difficult because that monkey on your shoulder is constantly telling you that it is true, so you believe it. You are letting something that an invisible monkey is telling you become your reality.

It sounds crazy doesn't it, but it is so much easier to just avoid something that is going to be hard, emotional or challenging and most of these things we 'believe' that are affecting our mindset are things that are going to be tough in some way. So, we avoid it which in turn makes us believe it to be true.

How we act in our life and our business is very much driven by what we believe we can achieve; our beliefs are driven by our mindset.

If you believe you cannot run a 10k race, then you probably never will.

If you believe you cannot have a successful business, then you probably never will.

If you believe you cannot create reels on Instagram, then you probably never will.

If you believe you don't deserve to be happy, then you probably never will.

I was chatting with someone recently, they were at the point of giving up as they just could not earn enough money to make ends meet, they had tried all the things. They had a great strategy; they had built a loyal audience and they had a great product to offer but they just could not get any sales.

They had been on numerous 'sales' courses and read ALL the books but every time they put the product out there, they got tumbleweed; their audience went quiet on them, and nobody bought, not one sale!

The reason she was not selling was nothing to do with the product, her audience, or her strategy; the reason she was not selling was her mindset. She told herself that she probably wouldn't sell anything, after all why would anyone buy from her, she had a negative mindset, so it was no surprise she did not sell anything.

Have you ever tried to do something that you do not believe in?

I have tried to lose weight on numerous occasions, but it never happens. I say I want to lose a bit of weight, but I do not believe I can do it, I do not think I can stick at it for more than a couple of weeks, after all I never have in the past so why should I this time. So, when the going gets tough, you got it I get going, going back to the cupboard for the crisps and chocky biscuits!

The only time I did lose weight (intentionally) was when I had a PT who kept telling me over and over again that I could do it, they spoke louder than that annoying monkey on my shoulder and I did it! Typically, this was just before COVID, and we all know the effect COVID had on our diets...but that's another story!

The principle here is that I know I could do it now so if I chose to lose weight again, then I know I can do it...and I will do it!

Your mindset is your set of beliefs, these beliefs are often there as a result of something that you have seen or experienced in your past, but they are things that very much shape your outlook on life and business. When you get stuck, mindset is likely to be part of the issue.

Do you know how your mindset is affecting you?

Let's have a look at five of the most common mindset struggles that we have and then we can have a look at how we can overcome them.

FIXED OR GROWTH MINDSET

If you have a fixed mindset, then you will not believe that you can be anything more than you already are. You will be stuck where you are, whereas those of us with a growth mindset will believe that with the right effort they can be whatever or whoever they want.

A fixed mindset would prevent you from learning new skills or committing to working with that coach you need to move forwards. It would prevent you from trying again if you failed. You will be saying 'I can't' a lot!

A growth mindset would mean you would try new things, you would push yourself to be successful as you know that the only way to grow is to keep trying! 'I will try' will replace 'I can't'

With a fixed mindset you are not going to move forwards, you will never give anything your best shot, you will remain stagnant and unhappy as you will never utilise your full potential.

MONEY MINDSET

Your money story will affect the way you deal with money, this is about how you handle money, how much money you will earn and how you feel about money.

Let me tell you a little story about me as I think it is a great way to show you how subconsciously your money story can affect your life and business without you even realising it.

A little earlier in this book, I touched on how my life become quite materialistic, about how the more I earned the more I spent. But what I did not tell you was the impact this had on my new business as I thought I would save that bit of the story for now.

In my mind money was bad, as it made me feel unhappy, it made me become a materialistic person that I did not like, I was replacing the things I could not have with 'stuff' I did not need. I thought that by having these things people would see me as something. Remember that comment the teacher told me...it was there again making me do stuff that I did not really want to do.

I wanted to see my family more, I could not do that, so I just bought them stuff instead. I wanted more interaction with people, but I did not have time, so I opened a retail store that meant I got to see customers (and work even harder!) I wanted to be abroad more, so I bought a villa in Spain, yes, I got to be in the sun, but I was still working!

When I launched my coaching business back in 2021, I did not actively sell anything for ages, I kept putting it off, I always had a good reason, I needed to finalise my brand, I needed to build my audience a little more, I wanted to do one more course first BUT the reality was I was afraid to sell anything as it may mean I earn some money which would make my life unhappy again.

You see I had worked so hard to get myself to a position that I was no longer doing crazy things with money, I was finally starting to be me and starting to enjoy life and the annoying monkey on my shoulder was telling me that if I sold anything I would go back to where I was, all my hard work would be lost.

I was letting my fear of earning money stop me from doing something I love!

Nothing brings me more joy then helping people on their own journey, it could not be further from the truth that I am doing it for the money, yes money is an essential part of life, but I have built this business with my purpose at the core...not profit so there was no way I was going to mess it up this time!

Once I realised this, I was able to do something about it, I was able to shift my mindset and now I love launching new programs, after all how can I help people if I do not offer them my services?

Your money story could be one where you have witnessed or experienced having no money or too much money but either way it can affect how you behave with money.

SELF-SABOTAGE

We are our own worst enemy at times and we are often the ones that stop ourselves from doing something, we tell ourselves we cannot do it, so we don't, we tell ourselves we should be doing more, so we do all the things which overwhelm us.

Self-sabotage can be conscious or subconscious; you know you need to write those social media posts, but you choose to scroll Facebook instead, that's conscious. But if you're not putting your posts out there as you believe they are not good enough, then that is subconscious.

IMPOSTER SYNDROME

Who do you think you are? I mean come on why do you deserve to be successful? These things sound familiar? Sadly, for many these are things they believe to be true. We allow ourselves to get in our own way as something tells us we do not deserve it.

Imposter syndrome can rear its ugly head in many ways and is often linked with self-sabotage or fear.

I used to believe that I could not go live on Facebook; I thought my voice sounded awful, I did not look as 'good' as the other coaches online, I would keep saying 'erm' and I would get my words muddled up.

I would write pages of notes, but still, I could not do it. I hovered over the go live button and I kept reading my notes, but I just could not do it. I stopped myself from doing something that I knew was the best way for my audience to get to know me, I knew it was a great way to boost engagement, yet I still stopped myself, I slowed my business growth down!

It is crazy, but it real; we let our mindset decide what our future looks like. We let that damn monkey win.

Are you a perfectionist? Do you feel that you cannot do something until it is perfect?

Do you think others are better at doing things?

When something doesn't quite go to plan, do you blame yourself, tell yourself 'I told you so'

Imposter syndrome is that nagging feeling that you will be found out, found out for not being good enough or for not deserving the success.

FEAR OF FAILURE OR FEAR OF SUCCESS

Fear of failure...I get that but fear of success, that sounds crazy, doesn't it? But it is totally a thing!

I was afraid of success; remember me telling you how I avoided selling anything as I was afraid of earning money as in my eyes money made me a bad person. It was totally irrational as my real fear was growing my new business to a stage that it took away my purpose, the money was just the thing I blamed as it was easier to see. But either way I had a fear of success.

Fear of failure often comes from something you have experienced. Maybe you have accrued some debt due to what you feel were bad decisions, maybe you have tried something before and it did not work, maybe you invested in a coach, and you still did not grow your business. Whatever it is somewhere in your mind you have decided that it will happen all over again, and that annoying monkey is there to keep reminding you of it.

 Happiness is a state of mind. You can be happy, or you can be unhappy"

— *WALT DISNEY*

I love Disney films and this quote is one that always rings true to me. We get to decide our own path, we get to decide if we want to be happy or unhappy, we get to decide what our future brings. It is our life so we can make it whatever we want it to be!

Back at the beginning of this chapter I told you that you can change your mindset, I also told you it wasn't easy, there is no off switch for the monkey, but it can be done, and you CAN do it!

The first thing you need to understand is what is your mindset, what is holding you back?

I want you to take each of the five mindset struggles we have just walked through, and I want you to think about how you feel you sit within them. Back in Step 1 you created a timeline of your own story, take a look back through that as you will often find things in there that have triggered a mindset struggle.

Now remember you need to be honest here, there is no point writing down what you feel is the right answer as a little secret here, there is no right or wrong answer.

If you want to change your mindset you need to firstly understand what your current mindset is and if you pretend it is something it is not, you will never change it!

I want you to move forwards and I can only help you do that if you are 100% true to yourself, nobody except you is going to see what you have written down, it is not something to be ashamed of, I have shared some of my deepest secrets with you in this book and I can only do that now as I have been honest with myself, it is not always a nice experience but it is so worth it and I am here to hold your hand.

Getting to know your own mindset takes time and it is an ongoing process. So please do not worry that you do not crack it straight away. Later in this book, we will talk about the ongoing stuff you need to do to maintain the balance and you can keep going over and over each of these steps as many times as you need.

So now you know more about your own mindset struggles and how they impact your life let's have a look at how you can shift them and how you can turn them into something more positive.

The big one; you need to accept that something needs to change, you need to be open to change and you need to be prepared for the rocky road ahead as change is unsettling for anyone.

For me the biggest shift in my mindset came when I started to journal. Every morning I spend five to ten minutes writing down how I feel, any worries I have, any ideas I have, my gratitude and my intentions for the day.

These few simple things have helped me to see things differently, they have helped me to appreciate the things that go well and to not see the hurdles as things I cannot overcome. Looking back to see how far you have come is a great feeling and a journal will give you evidence of that, in your own words.

I am going to talk to you more about journaling in Step 5, but I wanted to touch on it here as it really is a great way to help you with your mindset.

The next thing I want you to think about is flipping the switch; what I mean by this is turning the negative into something more positive, think about the impact of not doing something rather than doing it.

Let's go back to my fear of being visible; I told myself that my voice sounds awful, but let's be honest who cares, people want to listen to what I have to say not how I say it and so what if I say erm a lot so do lots of other people. If I say the wrong word, what is the worst that will happen? So, what that I do not have a perfect face of make up every day, so what if my hair is grey at the roots, who cares? All these things show that I am human and being honest, I am not and never will be a perfectly presented Instagram influencer, nor do I want to be so why does it matter?

If I had allowed my fear to win, I would not have been able to spread my message, I want to help women get the right balance in life and business and if I did not tell them how they can do that then how an earth am I meant to help them.

The impact of me staying hidden is more people having a miserable life and I do not want that! I am doing you a misjustice by letting my fear of visibility win.

Turn your negative beliefs into something positive; you can do anything you want to do, the only thing getting in your way is you!

You have to be patient as it takes time to see and feel the benefits of anything, you have to be consistent, even when it gets tough and even if you feel you are not building the momentum.

You need to face your fears head on; if something scares you, do it anyway...think about the worst thing that can happen, it will only be something that you are letting that monkey tell you is a problem, unless of course you want to do something really silly and dangerous, then you should seek professional advice first!

Get help, get the support you need. If you need more help then remember that is what people like me are here for, there is a whole wealth of support out there, coaches, mentors, friends, family, books, training courses, go and get it. Do not be afraid of asking for help, do not be afraid of investing in yourself. I say it again what is the impact of you not getting the support you need?

Baby steps, take one step at a time, you do not have to leap from never going live on Facebook to going live every day. You can go live in a private group with just you in it first and gradually build it up from there. You do not have to deliver a training session to a thousand people in a room, you can do it on a zoom call with two or three people first and build it up from there. Baby steps are all that you need but you need to start to take them.

When that monkey is sitting on your shoulder and telling you that you cannot do something or that it will go wrong if you do, tell him to do one. The monkey is not real, you are, and you are in control of what you do. Remember that you can do anything you let yourself do.

Always think of the impact of not doing something instead of what the monkey says will happen if you do it!

You are making great progress, you know your purpose, you know what is getting in your way of making it happen so now let's move onto the next step which is where you will start to put some plans into place to make the change.

3

THE LIFE PLAN

We have just spent the last two chapters talking about your wishes and aspirations, we have explored what you want your life to look like and what you want to achieve so now we need to look at how that becomes a reality.

The starting point has to be a life plan.

A life plan is going to give you a roadmap to make those dreams become a reality and as we move onto business planning in the next chapter, we will make sure that the two plans link together to give you that much needed balance we have talked about so much.

Did you know that you are 42% more likely to achieve a goal if you write it down?

As business owners we are told that writing down our goals is important, which is true, but how often are you told that life goals are far more likely to be achieved if written down too?

Just imagine you have 42% more chance of living the life you want, 42% more chance of making the dream a reality, why wouldn't you do it?

It was Christmas 2020 when I wrote down my first ever life plan, it was nothing fancy and it was nothing new but within three months of making this plan I had finally started to achieve my dreams.

This plan had made me feel empowered, it had given me the focus I needed and just by having it in writing I felt far more motivated to make it happen. I could tick things off and it felt so good each time I did, I had something to work towards and it felt real. It was real...my life plan was happening!

Before we go any further, I just want to touch on bucket lists, a bucket list is exactly what it says, a list of things you want to do before you "kick the bucket".

It is great to have one but in reality, for most it just remains a list of things you WANT to do. There is always an 'excuse' for why we have not done any of these things, can't afford, not enough time, nobody will do it with me, the list of reasons not to have done something is endless. I have used most of them, so I really do get it!

The reality is a bucket list is worthless without a plan.

In the words of Jim Rohn:

> *If you don't design your own life plan, chances are you'll fall into someone else's plan. And guess what they have planned for you? Not much."*
>
> — *JOHN ROHN*

I used to have a bucket list, nothing official, it was all in my head, but nonetheless it was a list of things I wanted to do before I die. It included living in the sun as I really do not like British weather, the rain and cold makes me miserable and all I want to do in winter is stay indoors.

Despite being very close at one point it was never going to become reality for me as I had no plan in place to enable it to happen, I was not proactively doing anything to make it happen, I was just sulking every winter that I was still here in the cold!

Do you get it? Have you got a list of things you want to do that never seem to happen? Have you ever wondered why?

In 2020 I started to create my life plan, which still includes being in the sun, but now I realise it not a permanent full time move I want, it is just the flexibility to spend the cold months there, it is just the freedom to come and go as I please.

By the time you read this book, my dream may well be my reality as I have finally been taking action to make it happen.

I still have a 'bucket list' of things I want to do, places I want to visit etc but now it is a vision board that forms part of my overall life plan, which is documented and backed by action.

 Without action a plan is just a dream"

We are going to build your life plan, but I want to start with your vision board.

A vision board is a great way to visually see your dreams. Having something visual to look at every day keeps you focussed on what you want, it helps to keep you accountable and keeps the dream alive.

Before we start to get creative, the first thing you need to do is grab a pen and paper as you need to brainstorm your dreams, you know you want a better life but what does this better life actually look like?

Some people like to think about the next five years, some like to think longer. There is no right or wrong timeframe. Mine takes me to retirement. You can decide what feels right for you.

The one bit of advice I give here, and I am not giving you this to spoil the dream, but I am going to say you need to keep it realistic, I mean it would be great to own a spaceship but let's be honest how likely is that, unless you are Elon Musk of course! What you don't want is a vision board of things you have no chance of achieving; it needs to be things that are going to push you but things you can achieve with the right action.

Not everything on this list needs to be huge either, mine ranges from getting my nails done every month to spending up to six months a year travelling. For some getting their nails done is such a small thing and not worthy of going on the list but for me, at the time, I was working 80-90 hours per week, so it was a huge thing as I had no time for self-care, but I love my nails looking pretty, it makes me feel so much happier. So don't assume anything is too small to be included...it really isn't!

When creating this list, you need to think about:

- *Your values*
- *Money*

- *Family and Relationships*
- *Health and Wellbeing*
- *Your Business*
- *Places you would like to visit*
- *Things you would like to do*
- *How you want to feel; think of affirmations or phrases that reflect this*
- *Things you would like to own*
- *People who inspire you*

Once you have all this stuff, you need to get creative. Personally, I like to get loads of pictures that reflect my vision and stick them to a huge board. If you prefer to use a scrap book or something electronic then that is fine too, I am not going to tell you how it has to be documented as this is about you, and what works for you, not me!

Just make sure when you have done it you keep it somewhere you can look it at all the time! It may sound a bit silly but looking at it regularly really does help to keep you motivated, it keeps the excitement real as it reminds you what you really are doing all this for.

Now you have this beautiful board covered in pictures and words that reflect your dream you need to make it happen and I am going to help you to create a plan that will do just that!

Without a plan and without taking action your vision board is never going to become your reality.

Before we get started, I just want to remind you that if at this stage you are having a little wobble, looking at the vision board and thinking I can't do that. Go back to step 2, shifting your mindset, and do some of the mindset work again. It is quite normal to feel a little nervous when you start to see your life planned out and as I said before mindset work is an ongoing thing.

Your life plan is going to help you to overcome some of these fears as it is going to give you a clear plan of action that makes big things not feel so big and scary. Your plan is going to keep you focussed on the end goal.

Your life plan is simply a list of actions that you will take to enable you to achieve each of the things on your vision board.

It does not have to be anything complex, but it needs to be SMART.

Specific: Each goal should be specific. For example, rather than 'make time for yourself' your goal should be 'get your nails done'

Measurable: How will know you have achieved it?

Achievable: Make sure your goals are realistic and possible to achieve.

Relevant: You need to make sure that whatever you have on the action list is moving you closer to your end goal. Think about your vision and ask yourself will this get me there?

Time-bound: Set an ambitious but achievable deadline.

Now I don't want you sitting there thinking this is all very complex, it really isn't. All you need to do is create a list of actions for each of the goals on your vision board that will make them happen.

The easiest way to get started is to group the stuff on your vision board, some of the things you have on there will require the same action, so it is pointless writing it down multiple times.

When you have grouped your dreams, you need to prioritise them, what are you going to work towards first?

Then you can start to break it down into things you need to do; some of this will cross over to your business plan which we will look at in the next chapter so don't worry about the detail for business goals right now as we will work that out later. All you need is a list of actions you need to take.

I suggest you start with a set of headings that are relevant to you, for most this will include:

- *Family and Home*
- *Business/Career*
- *Money and Retirement*
- *Health and Wellbeing*
- *Travel and Entertainment*
- *Hobbies and Interests*

I think it is also important to include your values and personal attributes on there as well, so they remain at the forefront of your mind.

I have a free template that you can download on my website to help you with this so go grab yourself a copy here:

www.emmahine.co.uk/free-stuff/

You don't need to build a five or ten year life plan as you have that on your vision board, what you need is a six or twelve month plan that is going to move you closer to your long term goals, of course you will tick some things off the list in that time, that is great but do not focus too much on the detail for everything or you are just going to get overwhelmed and then you will do nothing.

Remember this plan is going to need to be reviewed as it will change as the years progress, the important part is getting something drafted as it will give you the focus you need to put YOU at the top of your priorities list.

Life can be unpredictable, so you need to keep your plan flexible. You need to allow room for unforeseen things that may crop up.

My life plan changed at least three times in the first twelve months as I was still developing my 'thing'. I was still going through the process of fully getting to know me and what my actual dreams were. I had not given myself any focus for years, so I had no idea what I wanted my life to look like, I was still telling myself what I thought I wanted but for a while there it was not my dream, it was somebody else's that I thought looked good!

This is okay as it is still progress. I was still growing as a person so I was not yet being totally honest about how big my ambitions were, I was still letting the monkey on my shoulder tell me what I could and could not do!

Do not be afraid to be honest, do not feel guilty for wanting things for you. This is YOUR life plan and therefore it has to be what YOU want.

If you want to travel the world, if you want to eat at every Michelin starred restaurant in the UK or if you want

£100,000 in the bank now is the time to put it in writing and to set yourself some actions that will make it happen.

Remember if you take no action, it will never happen but if you try, it is totally possible!

Without my vision board and my plan, I would still be back where I was, miserable and feeling useless, instead here I am living life my way…it may not be perfect, and it may not be everyone's cup of tea, but it is my life, and I am doing it the way I want to do it!

You can do it too; grab your pen and paper and get scribbling…remember this is work in progress so do not stress that it's not perfect, progress over perfection wins every time!

4

THE BUSINESS PLAN

Whilst we work through creating your business plan, I want you to make sure that you keep your life plan at the forefront of your mind, pop your vision board up on the wall next to you and don't let your business plan steer you away from it.

It is very easy to get engrossed in the business stuff and to forget all the hard work you have just done finding your purpose and building it into a life plan but as I said right at the start of this book, if you want to keep the balance you have to manage both your life and your business hand in hand.

The reason my ecommerce business made me so unhappy was because I focussed purely on the business plan, so yes,

I had growth, but I was miserable as sin, and I do not want that for you!

If like me, you google everything I am sure you have googled 'What is a business plan' a million times already and no doubt you have read lots of stuff and thought what the hell do I need all that stuff for.

Well, the honest answer is you don't... some of that stuff is only applicable if you are looking for investors, applying for finance or that sort of thing!

A business plan can be lots of things, but it does not have to be complex, in fact the less complex the better in my opinion, as you are far more likely to do something with a plan that is actually understandable.

So, although I call this your business plan, which it is, I like to think of it more like the instruction leaflet for your newly purchased self-assembly furniture. It is something that you could muddle through without, but it is going to get you there much quicker and with much less stress and anxiety if you follow the instructions!

One thing I hope you are realising now is that I do not like to make business complicated; it is one of my core values, I used to find business so complex in the corporate world, why call something a fancy name and create a war and peace document that nobody understands or uses. If you only create things, you actually need you are far more likely to a) enjoy creating it and b) use the damn thing!

Now, before we get stuck in, I want to just make one thing clear, a strategy is a plan, they are the same thing. The only difference is the level they sit at. So, your strategy is your overall mission, it is what you want your business to achieve, it is the long-term vision, whereas the plan is a much shorter term set of actions that will start to move you towards your overall strategy.

Can you have a plan without a strategy?

Well in theory yes you can, but I would not recommend it. I would always recommend that you have an idea of the longer-term plan for your business as well as the shorter term as without the long-term vision how do you know that the short terms plans are taking you in the right direction?

It is the businesses with the long-term vision in mind that go on to succeed.

So, if you think back to the life plan section, we created your vision board first, that is your life strategy, which is the long-term plan. Then we built your life plan which is the shorter term set of actions that are going to get you closer to your vision board, one step at a time!

A business plan is no different, we firstly need to create the vision and then we can create the actions.

A strategy needs to cover off three things, your vision, your mission, and your values. All the detail below this will go into your business plan so it really does not have to be anything complex.

But do not mix keeping it simple up with not doing it properly. It may only need to be simple, but it needs to be thoroughly thought through as these three simple things should drive all the actions you have on your business plan and therefore if the strategy is not right, the plan will be wrong too!

And that really would be a recipe for disaster!

The Vision: This is what you want your business to look like. It is what gives you the focus for your business plans and what drives you to take the action you take. I have spoken a lot about your purpose, think of this as your businesses purpose, why does your business exist and what change is it looking to make?

When creating your vision, you need to really think about what YOU want your business to look like, remember this is your business and it needs to give you want you want as well as changing the world!

Think about your vision as the thing you are going to become.

The Mission: This is what you are going to do, the message you will spread, the solution you are going to provide for your clients.

This is how you are going to change the world and remember it has to be YOUR way!

Think about your mission as the things you are going to do today to make your vision become a reality in the future.

Your Values: This is what you and your business believe in and stand for.

You need to think about how you are going to do business, what are the key things that you are not prepared to violate.

Whilst creating your life plan, we touched on your personal values and as this is your business, I would expect there to be some crossover into your business values.

Your strategy is the heart of your company, and I cannot stress enough how important it is that you make sure it is aligned with your life plan.

These three things you are developing now will help you to shape everything in your business, from processes to recruitment through to the services you offer and the way you handle your client experience.

Without a strategy you will not have the focus you need; you are more likely to jump from one thing to the next and long term that is not going to give you the business you want.

If you have not already done this, grab your pen and paper and get going, create your strategy. Do not worry if it is not perfect from day one, like everything in business it will grow with you.

Now I have repeated myself several times, I hope you appreciate the importance of spending some time formulating your strategy before we get stuck into the fun part... the business plans!

Your business plan is the detail that sits below your strategy, it will pull together all the actions you need to take.

Some people talk about it as goal setting, which is right, but I think there's a little more to it than just setting goals and I am going to help you to understand all of that next.

Before we get started, I just want to remind you that your business is plan is shorter term than your strategy so for the purpose of this next exercise you are thinking about the next six to twelve months. You do not have to think about how to get yourself over the finish line today, but you have to create actions that take you in that direction.

Your business plan needs to cover off a few essential things:

Money - What is your financial target?

Products/Services - What is it you are going to sell?

Marketing - What will you be doing to make this happen?

Goals - What action will you be taking?

Metrics - How will you know you have achieved something?

Let's take a look at each of these things in turn so we can start to create your business plan. You may wish to do this a step at a time, or you may prefer to read to the end and then do it all in one go, it is completely up to you, there is no wrong or right way, just have the pen and paper ready!

But first let me just recap on setting SMART actions:

Specific: Each goal should be specific for example instead of saying 'build my audience' say 'gain 10 new people on my email list via my lead magnet'

Measurable: How will know you have achieved it? Using the example above you would know via your metrics as long as you track your audience numbers.

Achievable: Make sure your goals are realistic and possible to achieve. Make sure you have actions in place to make it happen, where will you be promoting your lead magnet etc.

Relevant: You need to make sure that whatever you have on the action list is moving you closer to your end goal.

Time-bound: Set an ambitious but achievable deadline. So back to the example I have used above add 'within thirty days' onto the goal.

Back to the business plan...

Money - I know you probably want to cringe at the thought of this right now as talking about money makes so many of us feel uncomfortable. But I am afraid it is time to get uncomfortable as you have to set yourself some money targets.

Back in the mindset chapter I told you about how my fear of earning money held me back and how it was not until I could turn this mindset around that I was able to finally allow myself to do the things I wanted and needed to make me truly happy.

Your money mindset is something that you need to constantly work on. At every stage of your business growth, you will face new money challenges so make sure you do not let it hold you back.

Your money target needs to include money you need to earn as well as money you want to earn.

The money you **need** to earn is how much money you need to cover all your business overheads like premises, insurance, stock and how much money you need to cover all your personal bills like your mortgage, your car loan, your electricity bill, your food etc.

I have a spreadsheet that includes all my personal expenses on it, so I know exactly how much money needs to go into my personal bank account every month. Before I created it, I had not got a clue, it was all guess work, and I was way off the mark. You have to think about everything you pay for, check your bank statement, and don't forget things you may pay for with cash like kids dance lessons and that sneaky take away you have twice a week!

The money you **want** to earn is for all those little extras you may want such as holidays, a car upgrade or a savings plan for the kids or your retirement. This is very personal, and you should not be embarrassed to say you want something. Think of that vision board you created back in the last chapter, what do you need to earn to make that happen?

Now I just want to put a little caveat in here, remember the SMART thing I mentioned earlier, keep that in mind and remember this is just for the six to twelve months so as your business grows your money goal can grow too. You want a challenging target, but it needs to be realistic at the same time.

Products/Services - You know your money target so now you need to know how you are going to earn it.

You need to think about the products/services you are going to offer, what will the price point of them be, how often will they be launched and how many of each are you looking to sell?

At this stage you need to sense check back to your money target, is it achievable based on the products/services you have to offer, or do you need to add more to your product suite or tweak the ones you already have.

Maybe you need to tweak your pricing structure or maybe you need to sell more of a particular product.

Remember your purpose here. For me, freedom plays a huge part in my purpose so at this stage I also do a little sense check against the time each of these products or services is going to take me as I do not want to create a business that is going to mean working crazy long hours, I have been there and do not want to go there again.

Marketing - Now you need to think about what marketing you will do to sell these products/services. Think about social media, emails, leaflets, PR, paid ads, whatever it is that you will do to ensure that you sell enough of the products/services to reach your money target.

I want you to think about the detail here, how many magazines will you pitch to, how many networking events will you attend, how many posts will you put on social media. Break it all down so there is clarity on the exact action you need to take.

Visibility plays a huge part in marketing so think about how you will make sure that you and your business are visible and most importantly how you will ensure you are consistent.

You also need to include a budget here, even if you don't have one. If you have no money to spend on marketing, then make sure you don't spend any but on the flip side if you have a budget make sure you spend it wisely on the things that enable you to reach your goals.

Goals - You now know how much you will earn; you know what you are going to sell and what marketing you will be doing to back it up so now you need to put some actions in place to pull it all together as without action a plan is worthless!

This is probably the biggest part of your business plan as it needs to be broken down into lots of detail, so you know exactly what you are doing and when. But in my opinion, it is the most fun part too so enjoy it!

For this part of the plan, I suggest you grab loads of post it notes and find a clear wall or space as a good old fashioned brain storming session is the best way to get all your actions pulled together.

Before you get stuck into your goals, I want to give you a few bits of advice that will help you with your goal setting

- Remember to keep them SMART
- Make sure that all your goals link to your strategy; if they are not getting you closer to where you want to be don't set them!
- Prioritise them; if you need to start earning some money in order to do some of the other stuff, make sure the initial goals focus on that!
- Don't set too many or you will just get overwhelmed and do nothing!
- Do not forget your purpose – keep the goals aligned to both your business and your life plan

Metrics - This is the final piece of the jigsaw, and it is the part that so many miss off.

There is no point setting lots of lovely goals and taking lots of action if you are not going to monitor what you have done. How do you know it worked? How do you know what you need to do differently or more of moving forward?

The answer is without something to track it against you don't!

Now I am not a mathematical person and the thought of lots of analysis does kind of freak me out but, it does not have to be anything complicated, trust me I don't do complicated, but I know my stats as I know how important they are to my business.

So, what is a metric?

A metric is a quantifiable 'thing' that is used to measure the success of a goal. I say thing as it does not have to be a number.

You need to have metrics to measure the success of everything you do in your business, so each of your high-level goals will need to be monitored so you can check at any stage what is going well and what is not going so well.

We will look at monitoring in more detail later on but for now we just need to set the metrics.

What is it that you need to track to ensure your business is going in the right direction?

Some key metrics will include:

Conversion rates - do you know the conversion rate at each stage of your sales funnel? Do you know the conversion rate on your website if you have one? Do you know how many calls you need to have with potential clients in order to get a sign up? Think about each of your touch points and make sure you have a metric to track it.

Sales/Profit - it is important to monitor your sales and your profit margin across all of your products/services, if like me you have a business (my ecommerce business) that makes this complex then look at averages.

Growth - you need to monitor your growth as a business, this will include sales and audience so think about social media followers, engagement, number of sales as well as mix of products/services that you sold

Client/Customer Satisfaction - a really important one is how happy your clients/customers are; happy clients will lead to repeat business and recommendations, so it is important to monitor this closely

Team Satisfaction - if you have one this is super important to monitor, a happy motivated team is worth its weight in gold so do not let this one slip!

That is your business plan done... well done for getting this far.

You know your purpose; you know what you want your life and your business to look like and you have both a life and a business plan in place that will make it happen.

Now what you need is to start taking some action so let's move onto Step 4 of my calibration system and let's get action taking!

5

BE PRODUCTIVE NOT BUSY

" *A plan without action will always be a dream*"

I t's true and you will hear me saying it ALL the time. This is the second time I have said it in this book so far!

I used to have lots of dreams, I dreamt of a life where I did not have to work eighty to ninety hours per week, I dreamt of a life where I felt happy just to be me, just to be in the moment doing the things I love.

It was not until I finally started to take the right action that this started to become reality.

You have your plans, your plans will make sure that what you are doing is the right thing to make your dreams become reality but unless you do the stuff, it ain't going to happen.

One of the biggest things, aside from mindset, which stops people taking action is time.

If you are not managing your time properly you are going to feel stressed and overwhelmed as you will have no focus, you won't know what you should be doing and when you should be doing it so you will be flicking from task to task and getting nothing done.

By managing your time properly, you will boost your productivity, you will be working on things that add value to your business and more to the point you will be doing them in a timely order.

You will start to see results; you will start to feel more positive as there is nothing better than that feeling of ticking something off the list...we all love that feeling of achievement, right?

Time management will also enable you to make better decisions. As I have already said you will be working on the right stuff, at the right time, so you will know what is right and what is wrong. You will not procrastinate as much as you will have spent the time doing the things that enable you to make your decisions. You will not just be making a decision in haste or with nothing to back it up. You will no longer feel pressurised to say yes or no to something as you will have had the time to investigate it.

It will help you to create a better work life balance. If you are not managing your time, you will take much longer to do anything, be it within your business or at home. If you do not have a schedule for the day, you will waste so much time thinking about what you need to do and you will spend much longer doing things than they should take, manage your time properly and you will get more free time, you will be able to differentiate between work time and home time. Life and business will feel so much more balanced.

In a nutshell time management makes you get stuff done which in turn will help to make you feel much happier and much more in control.

 I don't have the time"

First, let's bust this myth, come on be honest how many times have you said this? I know I have said it numerous times and I still do sometimes.

But the reality is it is a myth, we all have way more time than we think we have BUT we need to learn how to be productive not busy.

We can all be busy, busy thinking about all the stuff we need to do, busy running around like a headless chicken, busy stressing ourselves over the stuff that we do not have the time to do!

Now it is a fact that we all have different amounts of time, some people work as well as running a business, some people have young children that take up their time, some people have elderly parents they have to look after. What you need to work with is the time you CAN work.

When I first launched my ecommerce business back in 2006, I still had a full-time job in the corporate world, so I was out of the house from 7.45am - 6.15pm, even longer some days so I had to allocate my time to work on my business outside of these hours, yes it was hard, but nobody said this was easy!

Now is the time to stop this, we need to change the way we think, and we need to change the way we plan our time.

Poor time management is a habit, and a bad one that that, we can change our habits so we can change how we manage our time.

One more thing I would like to point out before we get into this, we CANNOT multitask, we may be able to do more than one task at once, but we will be giving each of the tasks a little bit less attention as it is impossible to actually give two jobs full attention at the same time. The science backs this up...go on google it, it is true! Now this may be okay when it comes to making lunch and watching TV but in business this is not okay as each task needs our full attention or why are you doing it in the first place!

So, what do we need, well lists are great, but they are not enough, we need to time-block.

Time-blocking is a little more structured than just compiling a list or just booking things in your diary.

It is taking your goals and breaking them down into tasks and then allocating them a time slot.

It is about agreeing your priorities for the week and making them non-negotiable.

It is about getting to know your own boundaries and more importantly it is about enforcing them too!

Time blocking is a game changer, and I am going to walk you through it step by step.

The first and most important part of time blocking is making sure you do it in advance, personally I spend an hour or so every Friday afternoon time blocking and planning the next week, but I know some people like to do it at the weekend, when you do it is fine as long as you do it in advance.

What I don't want you doing is turning up to work on a Monday morning with no clear plan of what you need to do.

You just need something that has hourly slots that you can draw on, so this could be a diary or calendar, you could create something on excel, you can buy PDF's that you can print. I have even published a specific time blocking diary. Link below for you:

www.emmahine.co.uk/shop/

The first thing you need to do is block out any time you cannot work, maybe you have a job as well so you cannot work between certain hours on certain days, maybe you need to fetch the children from school or you are having a day off, whatever it is you need to block this time out as it is given that you will not be working.

You need to make sure you block out lunch and breaks, self-care is something that I will harp on about all the time, I have been there and worked all the hours and forgotten to eat, but now I realise that it was unproductive and certainly didn't help me or my business. You have to build self-care into your life, or the scales will constantly tip out of balance.

I recommend everyone has a morning routine, be that journaling, be that spending time meditating or reading a book. Spending a bit of time before you start the day to set yourself up physically and mentally will make you far more productive. Personally, I love journaling but do what works for you and what you feel happy doing. Give it a try but make sure you don't give up after a few days, it takes time to change your habits and it takes time for you to feel the benefit of the change. Make sure you block the time out to do it.

Now you need to block out all those regular activities, the things you just do, these are the things that eat away at your time without you even realising, things like dealing with your emails, writing your social media and email content, setting your weekly goals, basically anything you must do every day or every week. I like to do these things at the same time every week, so I always bulk block them out for the month.

Remember to include any time you need to complete your personal development, be that courses, mentoring sessions, networking, or self-study.

The final piece of the jigsaw is breaking down your goals into tasks and allocating them the time needed to get them done.

Start with your weekly goals and create a list of what you need to do to achieve them, then allocate each of these tasks a time.

Make sure you leave some free slots, do not book yourself back-to-back as this allows no wiggle room. Life happens and things do not always go to plan so you need the flexibility to move things around.

In summary if you have to do something it needs to be allocated a time slot.

I want to share some of my top time management tips with you before we move onto the next chapter.

First of all, prioritising, this is something you need to get good at, so you need to work out what your priorities are. You should have done a lot of this work when you set your goals but now is the time to sense check it and to make sure that whatever you are doing it is bringing you closer to your goal.

For me I find 'eating the frog' helps so by doing the tasks I dislike most first it really helps my motivation, so first thing every Monday you will find me doing all the tasks that I find most laborious or most challenging. There is nothing worse than having 'that task' lingering around for a Friday afternoon so just get it done and you can forget about it for another week. Eat the frog!

Shiny object syndrome, we all get it! Be it checking your emails, your social media or being pulled to that 'thing' that you cannot resist, for me it is an invite to the pub.

Put your phone on silent, mute your email notifications and make sure you manage your clients' expectations. You do not need to reply to emails instantly, you do not have to answer every phone call, that is what voicemail is for. Remember if you always reply instantly that is what people will expect of you and the one time you do not do it, they will be disappointed, but people will wait a few hours or even longer for a reply if that is what they are told will happen.

Whatever you do, don't allow yourself to just do that quick task, it may only take a few minutes, but it is a distraction. It takes you far longer to stop start a task than it does to just get it done.

Stop doing those tasks that add no value to your business, or your life for that matter, spend some time making a list of all the stuff you do and if it is something you do for the sakes of it, scrap it. One of my quick wins when I did this exercise last time was ironing my clothes when I go away. I mean why do we iron our clothes, cram them into a suitcase to find they are creased again when you get there. Now if I buy something that needs ironing, which is rare these days, I just iron it when I am there. This is a simple thing, but you will be surprised how many of these obvious unnecessary things you are doing.

When you allocate a time slot to a task, stick to it. The trick is being realistic when allocating the slots but if something takes longer than planned, and some things do, then park it. Make a note of it and at the end of the day allocate another slot to finish it off later in the week or if you have a free slot later in the day then you can pick it back up then. This is why I said earlier it is important to leave some free slots.

I don't know about you, but my brain likes to throw ideas at me at the most unexpected of times, don't let this distract you, make a note of it so you do not forget and get back to the task in hand.

When planning your time, make sure you are splitting your time proportionately, you need to spend as much time working on your business as you do in your business.

On is things like planning and marketing, it's your growth strategy.

In is things like delivering a training session or making your products or doing your admin.

Get used to saying no, I do not mean say no for the sakes of it but if something does not fit with your values or if you do not have time to do something then do not be afraid to say no. It is not selfish to put your business first and it is not selfish to not be constantly at others beck and call. Remember why you started your business and make sure that you say no to anything that does not give you that, do not veer away from your purpose. It is your business, so you control what you do and when. Sometimes it may not be no, it may just be not yet!

I find that being somewhere quiet where I feel happy and comfortable makes me much more productive, so find or create a space where you can work that feels like your 'happy place'.

Make sure that you use your wasted time productively, so if you have to travel for work, use the train journey to deal with your emails. If you have to wait in the car whilst your child attends a ballet class, then use the time to do some breadcrumbing on social media.

Whatever you are doing you need to give it your full attention, so if it work, get work done or if it is play, play, and forget work! It is important to be able to switch off from one or the other; although I appreciate there is times where you may have to do both.

Do you use automation within your business? If not, then this is something you really need to consider, automation does not have to cost a fortune and it does not mean you have to replace people with robots, although if that works for you that is fine too.

For me there are a few things that I would advise all businesses to automate.

Social Media - Plan and write all your posts in bulk and schedule them; this makes it look like you are constantly online even when you are not plus you will get into a flow much easier doing multiple posts at once. This does not mean you cannot do the off the cuff posts, of course you can but at least you know you have lots of purposeful content going out regardless of what crops up!

Emails - Look at software such as mailerlite or active campaign to automate your emails; it not only ensures you meet the rules of GDPR, but it also makes the process so much quicker, and it gives you proper metrics to review.

Funnel - Having an automated sales funnel keeps the process streamlined and saves you loads of time plus makes sure that you do not miss anything, as nobody wants to miss a sale, right?

Now there is lots of other stuff that your business may be able to automate, in my ecommerce business we automated the fulfilment, the invoice production, the postage, the repricing and lots more too so spend some time thinking about what you could automate in your business.

My final tip is outsourcing; I believe that outsourcing should be something you consider in the early stages of your business.

It could be outsourcing something you cannot do or do not like doing like tech or bookkeeping, or it may be outsourcing something that takes up a lot of your time, but you can outsource relatively cheaply for example getting a cleaner or childcare.

Think about what gives you the best value verses the cost and do not be afraid of letting someone else do things for you.

So that is time management...it really is one of the most important business tips that I can give you, manage your time properly and everything will be so much easier, you will feel more in control, and everything will feel less of a battle.

Time blocking can work for everyone; but we need to be flexible as life happens and things do have to change. This is why it is important to keep free slots within your diary and to be realistic with the times you can and cannot work. Do not punish yourself if something gets in the way and you have to move things around; just stay focused and do some diary jiggling.

Remember, be productive not busy!

6

TIME TO DO YOUR THING

I have said this before but before we get stuck into this, I want to say it again.

 A plan without action is just a dream!"

You can have the best plans in the world but if you do not get stuck in and do the things that will make the plan become reality then it will just stay a dream, it will forever be something that you wish you had or you wish you could do or worst still something you see others doing and feel envious of.

You can have the life and the business you want; you have come this far you know exactly what that looks like, and you know exactly how that feels so let's take action and let's make it happen!

I talk about taking action a lot, but I want to clarify what it means, taking action does not mean doing anything, remember how I told you it was important to be productive and not busy, well that applies to action taking as well as time management. Taking action means doing the things that take you closer to your goal. The action has to be meaningful; it has to be the right action and it has to be taken consistently.

You have a kick ass plan, which means you know exactly what you need to be doing so let's go and kick some ass!

The first step in taking action is breaking that plan down into small bitesize chunks, little tasks that you can do each day to move you closer to that goal that you want to hit in six to twelve months' time. At this stage you need to be getting into the nitty gritty detail, making sure that you do not veer away from the plan or your purpose.

So, you set yourself a goal of growing your audience by two hundred people in the next three months, great! Now you need to think about how you are going to do that, what actual things are you going to do to make it happen.

Are you going to launch a new lead magnet?

Are you going to do some guest appearances online or on podcasts?

Are you going to get PR?

Whatever it is you need to work out the exact action you will take and when you will take it.

Don't forget to make sure that the actions you take are SMART.

Specific: Each action needs to be specific.

Measurable: How will know you have achieved it?

Achievable: Make sure your actions are realistic and possible to achieve.

Relevant: You need to make sure that whatever you have on the action list is moving you closer to your end goal.

Time-bound: Set an ambitious but achievable deadline.

So now you have broken your goals down into actions the next thing to think about is how you are going to make sure that you actually get them done.

Back in the time management chapter, I went over time blocking so first things first make sure that you take these actions and pop them into your diary. If you need a refresh on this, then go back to the Be Productive Not Busy chapter.

Accountability is something that really helps to keep us on track when it comes to taking action, so it is essential that you write your goals down. A written down goal is 42% more likely to be achieved than one you have in your head.

Remember me telling you about my first ever plan to tame my ecommerce business? Well, that plan was nothing new, it was something I had in my head and could have done years ago but I did not write it down, so I had no account-ability to make it happen, instead I carried on being unhappy and stressed for years.

If you are prone to giving up on your goals or to be constantly swapping from one thing to another, then the chances are you have no accountability.

If you need extra support when it comes to accountability, as many of us do, then there are a number of options for you to consider.

Get yourself a buddy, business buddies are great for accountability, I have a few and I absolutely love our monthly catch ups.

Find a group or a membership that feels right for you, there are loads out there that will include accountability, some incur monthly costs as they will come with lots of other benefits like 1-2-1-time, regular expert trainings etc but there are plenty of free groups that offer weekly accountability posts, my free group included. If you are not already a member, then you can join here:

www.facebook.com/groups/behappybesuccessful

Hiring a mentor or a coach, even if it is just for a few months until you get better at holding yourself accountable. Having someone in your corner to not only mentor you but to also push you along and make sure you take action makes a huge difference to how quickly you progress. I have invested in various coaches, and I totally know the benefit of it which is why accountability plays a key part in my 1-2-1 coaching programs as well as my group programs. If you want to discuss working with me then drop me an email, I'm always here to chat:

emma@emmahine.co.uk

One thing I want to be very clear on here, the action you take needs to feel right to you, there is no point googling how to grow your audience and just copying and pasting it into your diary. The actions you take need to fit with your values as you will just give up if you do not feel comfortable taking them. Do not forget your purpose which needs to remain at the core of every action you take.

How often do you talk yourself out of doing something?

For example, you set yourself a target of going live in your Facebook group once a week but when it comes to it you don't do it because one of the kids is unwell or you have not washed your hair, or you don't think you have enough information to share on the live.

We all have a great list of excuses up our sleeve that we can whip out at the drop of a hat when we don't fancy doing something, but they are exactly that...excuses!

To achieve your goals, you have to throw away that list of excuses, you have to take the action even if you are nervous or even if you have greasy hair, honestly nobody else cares...do the damn thing!

There is no such thing as the perfect moment, so please do not waste your life waiting for it to come along. I hate to be the bearer of bad news, but it will not come, you have to make it.

Whilst you are waiting, others are out there doing, so take the action now, make now the perfect time!

Which leads nicely onto my next tip, which is just do it, take the first step. It does not have to be the biggest action, it can be a small baby step, but it is a step forwards, it is a step in the right direction and honestly the more baby steps you take the sooner your dream can become reality and the more confident you will get to take the bigger leaps.

The snowball effect will kick in, but you have to put the first part of the snowball on the ground and give it a push until it is ready to roll on its own.

The first step is always the hardest and the scariest, but it is the most important one. It is the step that gets you going. Think about how exciting it is when your child takes their first steps, how excited you are when you puppy wees outside for the first time, the first one is always the most exciting so do it and celebrate the pants off it!

I find that setting myself three baby actions that I know I will achieve really help to get me started. It is a great feeling when you achieve something so what better way to get you motivated to take action than ticking off three actions straight away. They may only be small actions, but they are progress, and they are moving you closer to your goal.

Now one thing we need to get used to is things not going to plan, you will not achieve every goal you set yourself, some things will fail completely, others will not run as smoothly as you hoped, you will make mistakes along the way.

This is okay and is quite normal. It does not make you a bad business owner. We learn from our mistakes and the sooner we accept this fact the sooner we can move on.

Have you heard of the phrase 'failing forward'? Well, this is exactly what that is, it is an opportunity to use our mistakes as a stepping stone for our future success.

I will come back to this more in Step 5 of my calibration system, maintaining the balance, but for now I just wanted to set the scene, I wanted to get the point in that mistakes do happen, and it really is ok.

There are a couple more tips I want to share with you on taking action but before we go into those I just want to touch back onto mindset, as that monkey can be a right pain when you start to take action, so I want to quickly knock him off before he gets in your way.

As you start to take action and you start to see changes in your life and your business, you are going to feel uncomfortable, you are going to question what you are doing and most likely at times you are going to doubt it too.

This is quite normal, whatever stage in life or business you are at, as you change and grow it will feel strange. It does not mean it is wrong, it is just because it is unknown territory that you are embarking upon.

Back in January 2021, I sat and looked at my very ambitious plan to change my self-fulfilled ecommerce business to a fully outsourced business within three months and I very nearly changed my mind.

Seeing the plan written down and knowing that it could well have to be all undone if it did not work, knowing that I could suddenly lose lots of revenue that I may not be able to get back was terrifying. But what was more terrifying was the thought of continuing to work ridiculous hours, the thought of continuing to have no life and the thought of going back to that moment in time when I thought my life was not worth living.

Yes, it was going to be uncomfortable and yes it was going to be hard work, but you know that saying 'no gain without pain' well it is right. I could not carry on the way I was and the only way to make it better was to make huge changes, so I had to do it. It was time to put my purpose first and take my life back.

So, when you are feeling uncomfortable think about what happens if you do not do it, think about why you are making the change and think about how fabulous it will feel to be living the life and running the business you mapped out on your vision board.

You can do this; do not let a monkey win, you are stronger than you think. I did it, so you most certainly can!

Don't forget there are lots of tips and advice in the mindset chapter of this book so you can go back to that at any time.

The final two tips I have for you on taking action are consistency and looking after yourself.

Consistency is often confused with continuously, you need to remember your purpose here, if you do not want to be working every day then that is absolutely fine, it is your life, you get to choose but what you do need to do is take action consistently on the days you do choose to work.

I used to think that the only way to make my business a success was to work continuously, to never take a break and to keep pushing myself harder and harder. It reached the point where I was no longer productive, I was just 'working' I was not hitting the goals I wanted to hit but I could not see where I was going so wrong. I was working so hard and working such long hours, I was exhausted, and I was over-whelmed.

Now I work consistently instead, I work less hours, but I get so much more done in a day as I am doing the right things, I am no longer exhausted as I have all the right foundations in place and my brain is no longer total mush.

Have you ever noticed that the more consistently you show up the more engagement you get from your audience? It is not a fluke, people like consistency so good things happen when you are consistent.

It is essential that you take action consistently. Consistent action, even if it is just small action is progress, it will keep you motivated as you will start to see results. If you take a half-hearted approach, then you can only expect half-hearted results and that is not what you want...right?

Now, I am all about balance, it was what I teach my clients and it is what I believe is the key to you being truly happy and truly successful so I am not going to sit here telling you to be consistent and to do all of this stuff without making sure that you are taking care of yourself at the same time, that would just be silly!

Self-care is absolutely critical; you have to be mentally and physically in the right place to ensure that you are taking action in a way that will feel right and that will get you the results you want.

If you recall, I made it quite clear that when time blocking you have to build time into your weekly routine for you, this is not a nice to have it is a must have.

An exhausted business owner is not going to show up in a way that your audience need you to show up, an over-whelmed business owner is not going to take the action they need to take as they will not believe in themselves or the action.

In the last study I read 51% of small business owners have suffered from burnout, which is a huge figure and in honesty I am not surprised.

Self-care is essential so please make sure that you look after yourself, you are the most important thing within your business, so you need to treat yourself that way and you need to lose any feeling of guilt for treating yourself to an hour in the garden or a trip to the local beauty salon.

Now you have lots of fabulous tools in your toolkit, you are ready to start taking action, so it is time to move onto the final step of my *5-step Calibration System* which is maintaining the balance.

7

SPOTTING THE TRIGGERS

You should be so proud of yourself for getting this far, if you have been doing the things as you have read the book by now you have your vision, you have business and life plans in place and you know exactly what action is needed to make this vision a reality.

The fifth and final step in my calibration system is about how to bring this altogether and to ensure that you maintain the balance as let's face it life is not a bed of roses and there are always things thrown at us that knock us off balance.

Before we get stuck in, I want you to remind yourself why you are doing this as I think it is really important to keep that at the forefront of your mind when you are moving into unchartered waters, it helps to keep you focused on getting it done even when it gets tough and I am not going to lie to you it will be tough at times.

I started my journey because my life was totally out of balance, I was working all the hours and I was exhausted to the point that I just did not want to carry on. I hated my life, and I hated my business. I deserved so much more; I just could not see it as I was too busy.

The impact was much more than my mental health; my family never saw me and when they did, I was no fun, I had no fun left in me. I lost contact with friends as they got fed up with me letting them down. My business was also starting to feel the pinch as I was no longer working on the business just treading water to ensure the essential things happened. I did not want to be there, so I often hid at home away from the rest of the team, so I had no control over what was going on.

When your scales are not balanced everything is affected, it is just a matter of time. So, keep your reason for doing this in mind as it will be your motivation to keep going.

A little tip, I made some very simple notes at the front of my journal, so every time I felt it was too hard or had a little panic, I read the notes to remind myself why I was doing it. Without fail it put me back on track as I knew that I could not go back to where I had come from, I knew I needed to keep going.

So, grab your journal, open a google doc or whatever works best for you and make some notes. Write how you feel, what you want to change and why. Keep it somewhere safe and when needed read it. I used to read mine daily but nowadays I rarely look at it, but I know it is there if I need to.

My *5-step Calibration System* gives you all the tools you need to have the right balance between life and business, but it is not a magic wand that takes away all the challenges you may face.

There will always be occasions when your scales tip one way or the other, there is nothing you can do, buy, or create to stop this happening. But what you can do is learn to recognise it and to know exactly what you need to do to rebalance them as quickly and painlessly as possible.

We hear this phrase work-life balance banded around a lot but what we do not always understand is what it means.

This is not surprising at it means different things to different people. Your balance will depend upon your purpose, so what the division between work and life is for you may be totally different than it is to me.

Just because someone is happy working fifty hours a week it does not mean you have to, just because someone has a childminder to look after the children during the summer so they can carry on working it does not mean you have to. You should not be trying to be someone else, however amazing from the outside their life and business looks. This is about you and your purpose, and you will only feel in balance once you are doing it your way.

For me, a big part of my purpose is freedom, I want the freedom to work from wherever I want, I want the freedom to spend time with friends and family and I want the freedom to pick and choose who I work with. I do not want to answer to someone, I want the freedom to make my own choices.

So, when I think about my work-life balance I have to take into account my need for freedom, if I am spending too much time working, or I am not getting to travel or spend time with family then my scales are going to feel out of balance.

At times I will need to work longer hours, for example during a program launch, but that is okay as I know that once the launch is over, I will take some time off to do something I enjoy, which for me is normally book a holiday.

Keeping your purpose at the core of all of your plans, both life and business is critical; if you start to do things that do not link with your purpose then you are going to start to feel off balance and you are going to struggle to get yourself back into alignment if you do not nip it in the bud early on.

You know your purpose and you have created a set of life and business plans that have it right at the core of them; this is a great position to be in.

Step 5 is about how you make sure that you keep focused, it is about how you stop yourself from veering off from these plans and it is about knowing what to do when the scales become a little unbalanced.

There are three stages to Step 5 of my calibration system; rest, reset and resume. But before we delve into what they all mean I want to help you to understand how to recognise when your scales are out of alignment, I want you to know how to spot the signs as early on as possible.

Now, I cannot cover every sign, as there may be things that happen to you that are pretty unique to you but what I am going to do it go over the most common signs as you will relate to at least one of these, probably more.

A CHANGE IN SLEEP PATTERN

This is probably the most common reaction to being out of alignment; if something has upset you or something is worrying you then the chances are it is going to affect how you sleep.

Maybe you cannot get to sleep, maybe you wake up in the middle of the night and cannot settle back off, maybe you want to stay in bed in the morning when you are normally an early riser or maybe you have started to have random dreams.

You may think you are sleeping just as well as normal but still feel tired all of the time.

Whatever the reaction, if your sleep pattern has changed this is your bodies way of telling you that something is not right.

YOUR SPENDING HAS GONE A LITTLE CRAZY

Yes, this is a common reaction to feeling off balance, we often turn to spending money to compensate for things that we are not comfortable with. Often this is money you do not even have.

This is me, it is my knee jerk reaction, if I feel unaligned, I blow some money to try and make myself feel better. I may buy gifts for someone that I have not seen for a while due to being busy or I may treat myself to something I really do not need to justify working those extra hours and not taking the much-needed break.

There is a massive difference between treating yourself and what I call 'retail therapy' and it is important to spot the difference between the two. If your spending seems irrational, then the chances are it is.

YOU ARE HIDING AWAY FROM THE WORLD

Are you finding yourself cancelling social events or avoiding speaking to people? Maybe you have not been to the pub for a while, or you have stopped visiting your friend on a Friday lunchtime.

If you have stopped doing things that you normally do, if you have stopped speaking to people you need to speak to or even if you find yourself avoiding eye contact with a stranger in the street then it is time to look at why.

Hiding from the world is a common reaction to feeling fed up and overwhelmed and these are things we will start to feel if our scales are not balanced.

YOUR MIND WILL NOT STOP

Whatever time of day or night it is, whatever you are supposed to be doing, you just cannot stop your mind from wandering.

Maybe you cannot get something out of your head that is worrying you or maybe it is just thinking of total nonsense all the time but whatever it is if your mind is overly active and you cannot switch off, it is a sign.

YOU ARE EATING TOO MUCH OR WORST STILL YOU ARE NOT EATING AT ALL

You will have heard the phrase comfort eating; this could be overeating in general, or it could just be eating lots of foods that taste good as for a while there they make you feel happy.

Maybe you have always cooked healthy meals and suddenly you are living on take aways or going to the pub for dinner.

For some the reaction is not to eat, "I am too busy to eat; I'll grab something later" only you never do!

If you have had a change in your normal eating regime, then this is a sure sign that something is not right.

YOU STOP DOING SOMETHING YOU LOVE

It could be going to the gym or meditating or journaling, it could be absolutely anything but if you stop for no specific reason then this is something you need to explore.

It is common for us to deprive ourselves of things we enjoy when we feel unaligned, it is almost like we are punishing ourselves, not intentionally of course but nonetheless we are stopping ourselves from doing it.

When challenged why you are not at the gym this week, you will have a great excuse up your sleeve...but sit back and listen to your reason, is it real or is it just an excuse?

YOUR TIME OFF ROUTINE CHANGES

For most this is normally a case of taking no time off but for some it may be starting to take lots of time off.

Are you too busy to take a day off or book a holiday?

Are you are constantly looking for reasons not to be in the office?

YOUR TOLERANCE LEVELS CHANGE

Are you short tempered?

Are you snapping at people for silly things?

Are you normally a relaxed person but suddenly everything is pissing you off?

Maybe you are super emotional and everything and everybody is making you cry?

These are all things that tell you something is not quite right

YOU GIVE UP MUCH EASIER THAN NORMAL

Everything is hard work; nothing goes to plan so you may as well just give up...sound familiar?

Now, I am not going to sit here and say life should never be hard, sometimes it will. But if even the small things are starting to feel impossible then this is a sure sign that something is off balance.

Is quitting really the only solution? I bet it's not, it just feels that way when things are off balance.

EVERYTHING IS A MESS

No time or desire to clean or tidy anything away?

Has your home or your workspace become untidy or unorganised?

It is not surprising if you are working too hard, you are probably exhausted and the last thing you want to do before you collapse in bed is throw away last night's take away wrapper or recycle those empty wine bottles.

RELATIONSHIPS WITH LOVED ONES

When they say you take it out on the ones that you love, they are not kidding!

Life at home can become pretty rocky once your scales are out of balance.

Are you shouting at the kids all the time?

Is your partner driving you nuts and whatever they say you just can't help but snap at them?

Are you arguing over silly things?

Have you forgotten the last time you had fun at home and as for intimacy well that is a non-existent anymore?

Maybe you have stopped calling your friends and family as you find the conversation hard.

For many this is one of the early signs but sadly it is often the one that is ignored for the longest.

SELF-CARE

What is self-care?

I mean sometimes you are lucky to brush your teeth in a morning, right?

Seriously though if doing the basics in terms of self-care is getting hard never mind taking time out to relax in a bath or go to your favourite restaurant or beauty salon once a month then it is a sure sign that you have lost the balance.

NOT HITTING YOUR GOALS

If you are feeling out of alignment then at some point you will stop hitting your goals, for most people this is not one of the first signs so if you get to this stage then you have probably been off balance for a while.

Not hitting your goals is more of a secondary sign as the reason for not achieving the goals is likely to be one or a combination of the things, I have mentioned already but nonetheless it will happen if you miss any of the other signs.

As I said before there may be other signs for you and over time you will get to know what they are, but these are the most common ones that I have seen in my clients or experienced myself.

Did you recognise yourself in any of them? I bet you did!

In order to maintain your balance, it is essential that you learn to spot the signs, but it is even more essential that you take action when you realise something is not quite right.

Now, I do not want you to always assume that because you had a bad night's sleep everything is out of balance, it is quite normal for us to have an odd bad night's sleep but if it starts to become a habit or it starts to become an issue then that is when you need to be doing something about it.

Only you know what is normal for you so only you can recognise when it is starting to become an issue. But if others start to tell you that you are snappy or look tired then don't just brush it under the carpet as it is likely they are right!

8

REST RESET RESUME

S o here we are at the final stage of the process, it is time to rest, reset and resume.

At least every month I want you to follow this process even if you do not feel that anything is out of balance, if however, you recognise any of the signs in the previous chapter at any point in between then you need to do it straight away, do not wait until the next monthly review.

Remember I spoke to you about time blocking, well this is one of those regular activities you can book in bulk so make sure you get them booked in. Consistency is going to get you to where you want to be so much quicker.

Let's get stuck into this final piece of the jigsaw; the piece that makes sure you maintain your balance; I mean you have worked so hard to get it why would you want to flip back to unbalanced now?

REST

Before you delve into the reset part, I want you to take a little time to rest. This could be an hour, or it could be a day, but I want you to spend some time clearing your mind of the to do list. You need to get yourself into in a position where you can focus on reviewing the past month instead of thinking about the next one.

This isn't about reviewing; it is purely about getting your mind and body ready for reviewing.

I call it rest but this does not mean you have to do nothing, for some it might be easier to get yourself focused by doing something exhilarating or energetic, it is about finding your thing and doing it!

As a business owner, a mum, a wife, a daughter, a friend you have a lot of hats to wear, and it is not surprising that it can get a little overwhelming at times.

I have spoken to you already about self-care and I just want to take a minute again to emphasise how important it is to build self-care into your weekly routine. I am not here to tell you how many hours a week you should allocate for it as that really is personal choice but whether you think it is important or not you need to do it as I cannot stress enough how much more balanced you are going to feel if you have some 'you' time.

For me self-care is getting my nails done, it is watching TV, it is reading a book, it is going on holiday or for a drive in the car with my hubby. Self-care is personal and how you choose to do it is entirely up to you, but it needs to be something that makes you feel good and energised.

RESET

This is the bit I love; this is where you will review the past month and make sure that the next month is even better.

I do not want you just looking at your business goals here; this is a 360-degree review, we are here to live a balanced life remember so it is important that we review life and business plans at every stage. In fact, I want you to go even deeper than just reviewing goals. I want you to be looking at your emotions and your feelings as well.

The best way to track your feelings is to keep a journal; if you track how you are feeling, every day, you are going to find it so much easier to truly appreciate how you feel in comparison to the previous month. There are so many other benefits to journaling as well, many of which I have touched on in this book so if it not something you do already, give it a go.

Reviewing your goals is as important as setting them in the first instance. It is your opportunity to reflect on your progress, to analyse and make sense of the actions you have taken whilst making sure that they are still the right goals for you and your business moving forward.

Goal setting is exciting, it is when you are most likely to imagine yourself living this new life you have planned out, it is when you feel the most motivation to make it happen so by reviewing them regularly you are going to keep this excitement going.

Even the best of action takers can get bored especially if the goals are not quite hitting the spot so if you do not review your goals regularly then the time will come when you give up; it is not a matter of if, it is a matter of when.

A common mistake made by business owners is not reviewing their goals, I did not review mine for years which meant the goals I had were totally out of date and taking me in the wrong direction entirely, so it is no wonder the business and life I had were not the ones that I wanted.

Go back to that moment where you closed your eyes and imagined yourself living the life you wanted, you felt the emotions and the energy that this new life gave you.

Remember the mantra I asked you to repeat?

 That dream is going to be my reality"

Now is the time to assess if you have moved closer to that 'dream', now is the time to make sure that the action you are taking is touching the spot, that it is making you start to live and breathe at least some of those emotions you felt at that moment.

Although some of this review will be based on non-tangible things like how you feel; much of it will be based on assessing the metrics that you put in place for each of your goals, the measurable piece of the SMART goal setting technique that I showed you.

There are a few questions that I always ask myself for each of the goals I have in place:

- *What went well?*
- *What did not go so well?*
- *What have I learnt?*
- *How do I feel?*

Remember I touched on 'failing forward' earlier in the book, now is the time to put this into action. In fact, now is the time to go one step further and start 'failing fast and failing forward' In simple terms this means learn by doing, make the mistakes, learn from them quickly and use the learning to shape the next action you take. No looking for excuses why something went wrong, just learn from it and move on!

Always remember that you can learn from things that went well as well as things that did not go quite so well, it is important that you take learnings from both.

Make sure that you do this for not only your business goals but your life goals as well. You are aiming for a balanced life, you will only get it and maintain it, if you look at the two things hand in hand, you cannot do one without the other, it is as simple as that!

One question I am often asked by my clients is how do I track progress? Do I need a fancy scoreboard or something super technical to track progress?

The answer is no you do not need anything complex BUT you do need something. That something could be a spreadsheet, a google doc, a planner or it could be a specific piece of software like a Trello board or Asana.

My recommendation is whatever you use to write down your goals in the first instance is what you use to track progress. No matter what method you use the important thing to remember is that it needs to work for you. If it is overly complicated or does not look aesthetically pleasing to you then you are not likely to use it. I would rather you stick with a basic spreadsheet than try and use something that that will stress you out. If, however you are a tech geek then go for it, there are some fab apps out there.

Asking yourself the questions and logging the outcome is not enough though, you need to do something with the results.

If something did not go well, you need to look at why. Did you not have the right resources? Did you not take the action needed? Did something unexpected get in the way?

On the flip side if something went well, are there things that you did that you could do more of? What did you do differently with this goal than the one that you did not quite achieve?

This is not a beat yourself up for not achieving something exercise, I get that, we all do it!

It is about getting a rounded understanding of whether or not you are on target and if you are not, it is a case of finding out why so you can adjust the plans moving forward. It will become a beat yourself exercise if you keep missing the target, so it is important to review and under-stand why you are missing it.

Maybe you are setting unrealistic deadlines or maybe you are not taking the right action, this is your opportunity to explore all of these things to stop it becoming a problem.

Now you have reviewed your goals and you know exactly where you are up to, the final stage of the reset is to sense check the outcome of last month against the goals you have in place moving forward.

Are the goals still relevant?

Are you still on track to achieve them within the timeframe you originally set?

Do you need to make any changes?

What additional support do you need?

This is your opportunity to make adjustments to your plans, it is the whole point of reviewing, you are trying to make sure that what you are doing is the right stuff, that it is getting you closer to those long-term visions you have for your life and your business.

It is not about making changes for changes sake; if things are still on track, then that is great, but you should not be afraid to make tweaks, circumstances change, things do not always go to plan.

Goal setting is not a one-time process, it is something you have to constantly review, tweak, and change so do not be afraid or disappointed when you have to change your approach.

I know I said that was the final stage of the reset stage, and it was but one thing I want to add here is make sure you celebrate! Celebrate the pants off the things you achieved, even if it is something teeny, it is a win, it is a step closer to your goal and it is 100% worthy of celebrating.

You can choose how to celebrate but remember to share your wins, be it with your clients, your business buddies, your coach/ mentor, your family, or friends. It feels so good to celebrate so make sure you do it!

RESUME

Now you have reviewed everything, and you know exactly what tweaks you need to make to your plans for the next month it is time to get back to it, take yourself back to step 4 and let's start to take action all over again.

Before I wrap it all up...

Let's take a few minutes to remember why we are doing this, why you chose to read this book and why it is so important that you start to make these changes right now.

Throughout this book we have looked at how it makes you feel to not have the right balance between life and business, we have looked at the emotions and feelings it has given you over the last few months or maybe even years.

I am going to be blunt here, living an uncalibrated life is a pretty shit one; you deserve better; you can have better; you will have better if you take the right action.

This is your life, and it is your business, so you get to choose exactly what that looks like. No more 'making do' or 'doing it for someone else'.

I want you to do it for YOU, I want you to do it YOUR way and I want you start living a calibrated life.

I did it...you can too!

9

LET'S WRAP UP

What a journey you have been on. I warned you it would be emotional! I am so proud of you for getting to the end.

I have taken you right through my 5-step calibration system and along the way you have learnt so much and by now you have all the tools you need to create a balanced life and business, but it is more than that you know the steps you need to take to maintain it as well.

At the beginning of this book, I made a promise to you. I promised you that you can realign your life and your business, you can change things and you can find the right balance.

I stand by that promise, if you follow all the steps, I have taken you through then you can do it.

Remember I asked you to make a promise to me too. I asked you to promise to commit to taking the action and to trust the process. I also stand by that; you have to do the work if you want to make changes and I know you do or you would not have come this far. I know you now, you are not a quitter!

My *5-step Calibration System* has taken you through ...

Finding Your Purpose - Finding your true purpose in life and in business, without this you will not know what balanced looks like, you will not know what is missing and why you feel so out of alignment.

This step can be emotionally draining; but it is the part that sets the foundations for everything else you do so it really is an essential step to ensure you become and remain in balance. It is the step so many skip and that is why so many people are out of alignment, overwhelmed and pretty fed up!

You explored your life story, you got to know what you like and what you dislike, you learnt about the legacy you want to create, and you took some time to imagine yourself living your amazing new purpose driven life.

You need to keep hold of that dream as now is your time to make it your reality!

Shifting Your Mindset - You need to have the right mindset to move your life and your business forward.

During this step you explored how your mindset can affect your ability to take the action you need to take, you got to know some of the mindset barriers that you may face, and you learnt some techniques to help you control them and to shift your mindset around.

Keeping your mindset in shape is going to be an ongoing process so make sure you some back to this step time and time again.

Don't let that monkey tell you anything else...you are amazing, and you can do this!

Setting The Roadmap - Knowing what to plan and when is really important, knowing how to build your purpose into these plans is the key difference between balanced and not balanced.

This was a huge step; you created a vision board and a strategy then you backed them up with a life plan and a business plan. You built a set of plans that will enable you to move forwards in a way that will keep you balanced.

The key ingredient here was making sure that your purpose was at the core of your plans.

Your life, your business, you get to choose what it looks like!

Taking Action - You know what you need to plan but what do you do with this plan once you have it?

You have explored time management in detail, and you have taken your plans and turned them into bite sized actions that you can take each day/week. You are now ready to start ticking things off and getting it done.

A plan without action is just a dream remember and you don't want a dream... you want reality... so take action and make it happen!

Maintaining the Balance - To keep that 360-degree legacy on track you need to understand what it looks like; you need to constantly review it and you need to recognise when things are not quite on track so you can readjust your scales a little.

You explored the triggers that are likely to occur if your scales are tipping out of balance and you discovered Rest, Reset and Resume which is a critical process to follow to ensure you maintain the balance.

A balanced life is a happy life, I created mine and now you can too!

10

FINAL RAMBLINGS

One final thing I want to say before drawing this book to a close is remember that this is not a do it once exercise, you have to keep doing it.

I am still on my journey yet here I am doing things that scared the life out of me only a year or so ago. Writing this book, is definitely one of those things I dreamt of but did not have the confidence or know how to do. Had I not followed my own *5-step Calibration System* I would still be dreaming of it right now, yet here I am writing the closing lines of my book.

I invested in myself, and my life has changed drastically, now it is your turn!

Thank you so much for reading my book, I truly hope that it has helped you in some way and that you can take at least some of the learnings from it to enable you to rebalance your scales of life and business.

I feel so blessed to have been able to share not only my *5-step Calibration System* with but also my journey. I will be honest it has been a bloody scary process as not many people (until this went to print) knew much about my life yet it is now all written in here in black and white for everyone and anyone to read.

I shared my story as I believe it will help others, you included, to see that there is no such thing as a lost cause, there is no such thing as being destined to be a nobody.

If you want to be somebody, then you sure as hell can be.

I did it, you can too!

I would love you to let me know how you get on with your journey, I am here for it all, the snot bubbles, the tantrums, and the celebrations too!

Massive well done for sticking with this process, I know how tough it can be, but I also know how beneficial it is too.

Keep in touch and do not forget your purpose...ever!

Your life; your business; your choice!

Big hugs

Emma xx

ABOUT THE AUTHOR

EMMA HINE

Emma Hine, aka The Calibration Coach is on a mission to help women in business rebalance their scales and find an equilibrium between life and business. Freedom and quantum success should fit hand in hand and women need to be able to find both, on their terms.

Emma has reignited her life and entrepreneurial passion, after being a 7-figure business owner ready to give up on everything, including herself, just a few short years ago. She now helps other women start and grow businesses that puts them first in a bid to reduce the amount of burnout and anxiety often attached to being self-employed. We need to focus on purpose before profit but most importantly you and how you want your life to look.

Having felt that ending her life was the only way to make things better after creating a monster that she hated and resented, Emma is passionate about ensuring women in business love what they do. Because we get to do it our way, and Emma is a shining light in this space, after now completely transforming her 7-figure business to one that no longer drains her as well as launching her heart led coaching business fuelling her passion to help others.

From being told by a teacher that she'd be a failure in life, and becoming a mum at sixteen, Emma could have taken a very different path in her childhood and with her mental health challenges and anxiety driving her life for many of her adult years. She could have given up completely - but Emma is no quitter. Her resilience and determination to create a life worth living has seen her find her true focus and she's excited to play her part in creating some rebalance in the lives of stressed out, unfulfilled businesswomen globally, putting happiness back at the core of their consciousness.

With a range of services including 1-2-1 coaching programs, group courses and in person events Emma has created a suite of services that ensure she can help women at all stages of business. If your life and business is out of balance, Emma's mission is to offer a service that can and will help you to thrive.

Emma's main driver in life and business is freedom, she loves to travel and is often spotted eating pizza with a sneaky glass of chardonnay in her hand – it would be rude not to.

Beyond supporting her clients, Emma is a wife, mum to three grown up girls and Nanny to three gorgeous grandchildren who she totally adores.

Emma lives by her motto: *Your life, Your business, Your choice!*

WORK WITH ME

If you would like any more support now or in the future then I would love to work with you, so to help you find out how we could work together I have included all my links below for you.

You can join the *Be Happy Be Successful* (BHBS) community, this is my free Facebook group for women in business, it is all about connection and supporting each other to rebalance the scales of life and business. It is great fun, and I would love to welcome you in.

www.facebook.com/groups/behappybesuccessful

I offer a range of 1-2-1 services as well as group programs and in-person events and more, the best place to keep up to date with what is currently available is to visit my website.

www.emmahine.co.uk

Or you can simply drop me an email and we can have a chat.

emma@emmahine.co.uk

Come follow me on Instagram, on there I share lots of snippets from my life as well as business stuff so if you want a giggle at my latest attempt to do something energetic or you want to join me on my travels then come and give me a follow.

You will also find me:

instagram.com/emmahine_the_calibration_coach

linkedin.com/in/emma-hine

ACKNOWLEDGEMENT

Is it wrong of me to say this is one of my favourite parts in a book, and it is most certainly the part I was most looking forward to writing?

I think it is because it is where I get to thank everyone for being so amazing and for helping me on my journey. I love watching awards ceremonies too, it fascinates me how many people there is to thank but it also makes me appreciate that we all need cheerleaders, we all need support and saying thank you is so special.

So here goes...my totally unprepared, from the heart, thank you speech.

First of all, Lisa Johnson, Business Strategist. I became part of Lisa's world right at the beginning of my journey and I know she will not realise it but without her I do not believe I would have continued my journey. Lisa you are amazing, and the online world needs more people like you, keeping it real and keeping it honest! Thank you from the bottom of my heart for helping me to change my life.

Next up is Nicki James, Brand Strategist. This woman literally took me, shook me, and spat me out as a totally new woman. She made me cry, she made me spit my dummy out on more than one occasion and she took me to places that I literally hated as they were so far away from my comfort zone, but she always did it from a place of love. She knew that Emma was in there, hiding and her mission was to get her out and boy did she do it! Thank you, Nicki, I am forever grateful to you and so happy to still be working with you.

Abigail Horne and her team at Authors and Co. Abi gave me the confidence to make my dream of being an author a reality, without her little push I may have chickened out so thank you so much for believing in me. Your team make the process so easy and dare I say it after all my 'I cannot do this moments' they made it fun too! Thank you!

I also want to thank my hubby, Adrian. He really has been my rock; he literally saved my life, and I am truly grateful that he is by my side whatever life throws at me. I do not believe I could love anyone more if I tried...and he knows it as I tell him all the time! Adrian, you are the man of my dreams, thank you from the bottom of my heart for choosing me and for sticking by me...even when I made your life a misery. I love you!

Then there are my girls, Becky, Charl and Emily. Life would be pretty boring without these three to keep me busy. I know I have not always been the perfect mum and you have had to see me in some pretty messy states for which I am truly sorry. But that is the past and we have years ahead of us to make up for lost time. No more "I'm too busy" from me! I love you all more than you will ever know. Thank you for being the best children, I am so proud of the women you have become.

My BHBS community, you guys' rock and I absolutely love having you in my world. You have been there throughout my book writing journey and have helped to keep me motivated even on the days where I wanted to give up, and there has been a few of those days! We really are a community and we really do support each other.

I know there will be specific people I have not mentioned but I realise I cannot thank everyone personally as so many people have been part of my journey and this book writing process, so I want to do a little catch all, thank you to:

My mentors and coaches for supporting and pushing me.

My audience and clients for being so loyal and so bloody amazing.

My business besties (you know who you are!) This time eighteen months ago I knew none of these ladies yet now we are the best of friends. I feel lucky to have got to know you all!

My friends, thank you for sticking we with me and for helping to keep me on track!

Finally, there is you. Thank you so, so much for reading my book and for being part of my world, it really does mean so much to me.

Printed in Great Britain
by Amazon

21254351R00092